First published in the United States of America in 2018
By Rizzoli International Publications, Inc.
300 Park Avenue South
New York, NY 10010
www.rizzoliusa.com

Originally published in French in 2017 as *Pomme* by Editions de la Martinière
©2017, Editions de la Martinière—une marque de la société EDLM
www.editionsdelamartiniere.fr

English translation by Carmella Abramowitz Moreau

Cover design by Kayleigh Jankowski

2018 2019 2020 2021 / 10 9 8 7 6 5 4 3 2 1

ISBN: 978-0-8478-6220-7

Library of Congress Catalog Control Number: 2017941126

Printed in China

CHRISTOPHE ADAM

APPLES

SIXTY CLASSIC AND INNOVATIVE RECIPES
FOR NATURE'S MOST SUBLIME FRUIT

PHOTOGRAPHY
LAURENT FAU

STYLING
MARION CHATELAIN

TEXT
SOPHIE BRISSAUD

RIZZOLI
NEW YORK

New York Paris London Milan

Apples

This cookbook is all about apples, nothing but apples, in every form and shape imaginable. In my recipes, I put this fruit through every transformation a pastry chef–and food lover–can imagine.

Apples are the fruit most widely grown and consumed in the western world. The apple is also the basic fruit of every pastry chef, the one grandmothers and mothers turn to first when they bake for their loved ones. In fact, it's the go-to fruit for most homemade tarts. Sad to say, the number of regional varieties has diminished, but there is still a wide range to choose from. You can select from those apples generally available in mainstream stores and the heirloom varieties you might stumble upon at a farmers' market or while on a walk in the country.

This book of apple recipes will open up new horizons to you for a familiar, appealing, easy-to-find, and easy-to-bake orchard fruit. We may think we know everything there is to know about apples, but there are surprises in store. The fascination grows when you learn that there are some twenty thousand varieties of apples around the world, each with its distinctive features and uses. There are dessert apples, cooking apples, apples for hard cider. Apples have varying degrees of crispness, softness, firmness, and juiciness; they are sweet or sour, or both. Their palette of colors ranges from grey to red, with hues of green, yellow, and orange. The recipes here include all the textures that the art of pastry-making can imbue: soft, crunchy, smooth, liquefied, or quite simply, crisp to the bite.

I have included classic recipes such as apple upside-down cake in its well-known French version of Tarte Tatin, traditional apple pie, candy apples (*pomme d'amour*, "love apples" in French), apple cheesecake, and several types of tart, but I have extended the repertoire to create more unexpected recipes, both from home and abroad: a trompe l'oeil apple ice cube, peel tempura, apple gratin dauphinois, Hungarian apple soup. A few of France's finest pastry chefs, like Christelle Brua, Laurent Jeannin, and Cédric Grolet have entrusted me with some of their secrets to share with you.

There is a brief guide to apples by way of introduction, and for each recipe, I will accompany you, step by step, to help you choose the most appropriate apple varieties. Please join me in discovering all the potential of the fruit that is both the stuff of legends and part of our daily lives.

A Selection of Apples

For most recipes, you will have the choice between several varieties of apple—hardly ever is only a single one appropriate for a specific dish. For desserts and pastries, we have decided to categorize apples according to their taste and texture: sweet or sour, firm or soft, dense or juicy, also taking into account that some apples soften when cooked and others hold well.

Of the several hundred varieties that grow in France, and 2,500 in the US, available at supermarkets or small village markets, at fruit and vegetable stores, or picked from the garden, we will only mention a few. We include many of the most common apples, others that are somewhat unusual, and a small selection of French heirloom apples.

A last but essential point to bear in mind: apples are seasonal. Apples that can be bought year-round tend to be available because they have undergone some chemical treatment or other. Some of the early apples are ripe to be picked late in summer, while most are ready in fall; still others reach maturity in winter. And almost all can be stored until the following spring. When and whether you can find them depends, of course, on how well they keep.

American Reds [7]

Firm (sometimes mealy), crisp, fairly juicy, sweet, not very flavorful, translucent flesh, shiny skin. An apple to slice or to bite into.

With the Red Delicious that was used to make hybrids including Starking Delicious, Strarkimson, and Red Chief, the Reds are all similar. They have a dark red skin, a truncated cone shape (narrower at the base than at the top), and gleam like well-shined shoes. They are the archetypal apple to give to the teacher in the morning. Since they were developed, they have been classified—and wisely so—as apples for intensive farming and decorative apples for the fruit basket. Nevertheless, some traditional and organic apple farmers manage to bring out their true nature; these are crisp, sweet, and juicy. Red Delicious has been found to be the apple richest in antioxidants (quercetin), so if you happen to find organic Red Delicious, simply wash them and bite on them with the skin. All of these apples are best eaten raw; they are unsuitable for cooking—and even more unsuitable for baking in pastry.

Antarès®

Firm, crisp, juicy, flavorful, good to eat and cook with.

This is a recent variety dating from 1980. It has a rustic appearance and its skin is marbled, with red and orange hues, similar to that of the Pippin and other heirloom varieties. The flavors of this versatile apple are a good balance between sweet and sour. The Antarès® is in season from September to early April.

Belle de Boskoop (Boskoop) [11]

Firm, very tart, moderately juicy, and crisp. Good for all desserts and all other culinary uses. A cooking apple.

This is a traditional fall Pippin that originated in the Netherlands in 1856. Its distinctive skin is slightly rough, grey-green on a red background. This firm, large-sized apple is very tart, and, because the flesh has little juice, it is not as good as many others when eaten raw. However, it holds its shape when cooked and is multipurpose for baking. In fact, it is an ideal tart or pie apple: simply ensure that its sourness is balanced. It is very rich in Vitamin C, containing double the amount found in the Golden Delicious, and it keeps well.

Braeburn

Very firm, tart, juicy, and crisp. Good for eating, juicing, and baking.

This fall apple, with its brick-red skin and green and tawny striations, comes to us from New Zealand. It is usually oblong or conical and generally lopsided. Since Braeburn apple trees are very productive, it is a variety that apple producers like to cultivate, and it is found worldwide. .

Chantecler [10]

Firm yet yielding, with a good sweet-sour balance, juicy, crisp, with a pronounced flavor. Good to eat raw, but also good for baking and savory cooking.

This apple is known, more precisely, as the Chantecler-Belchard. It is yellow and ripens fairly early–it is picked early in October. It resembles both the Golden Delicious–with a little more roughness–and the Reinette Clochard (also from France, but known since the 1880s) and there's a reason: it is a hybrid of the two varieties. It is round, but slightly flattened, with a skin of one hue that is often scabbed with small grey dots. Those who find the Golden Delicious a tad impersonal but like its firm texture will appreciate the Chantecler. It is well-flavored, excellent raw, and well-balanced. An apple that holds its shape when cooked, it is one of the most suitable varieties for both baking and cooking.

Cox's Orange Pippin

Firm, juicy, sweet, flavorful, and excellent for all purposes. Good in tarts, particularly upside-down apple tarts (tarte Tatin).

This English apple, considered as the classic English-style apple, dates back to 1825, could almost be considered an heirloom variety, and it is from the Reinette category. Its color is orange, it is juicy and firm and its sweetness has pear-like notes. It is the only variety of apple whose seeds audibly rattle when the fruit is shaken. All in all, it is a wonderfully versatile apple. Currently a little out of favor in the general distribution circuits, it can often be found at farmers' markets.

Cox's Orange Pippin apple trees have very particular climate needs and thrive best in cooler summers; they can be found growing in Nova Scotia, New York, and the Pacific Northwest.

Elstar

Crunchy yet soft, sweet, a good dessert apple, also good for juices and for applesauce.

The underlying skin color is yellow, spotted or striated with red. One of the early apples, picked in September, it is easy to find in supermarkets, where it is never quite as good as its cousins grown on small or organic farms. It was bred in the Netherlands in the 1950s, and is perfect as a dessert apple: sweet, crisp, and refreshing. Applesauce made with Elstar apples is always delicious. If you are baking with Elstars, keep in mind that the flesh softens: to make the most of this attribute, use them in cakes and fritters rather than in tarts.

Fuji [1]

Firm, juicy, sweet, and crisp with a fragrance of rose. A dessert apple, also used to make juice and hard cider.

Developed in Japan, where this variety represents 80% of apple consumption, it is also used to make hard cider. China too is now a large producer of Fujis, and the finest examples of these apples are to be found in Asia: sizable, flavorful, and crisp. Fuji apples, which are harvested in the fall, are light red or pinkish and their flesh ranges from white to greenish yellow. The trees must be grown with the utmost care to ensure their delicious flavor, otherwise they are of little culinary interest. Good-quality Fujis are perfect dessert apples and make excellent juice.

Gala and Royal Gala [8]

Firm, juicy, sweet, crisp, with a fragrance of yellow flowers. Best eaten raw as a dessert apple, but can be cooked.

Gala and Royal Gala are synonyms for the same apple. They come to us from New Zealand and have been commercially distributed in Europe and the US since the 1980s. With its season starting in September and ending in May, this early variety has been a huge success, and it's easy to understand why: it is round, firm, juicy, and crunchy, and its yellow, slightly translucent flesh has a delicious taste with notes of vanilla. Its aroma is reminiscent of yellow roses or freesias. It is also an extremely attractive fruit, with a shiny yellow skin finely striated with red. Should you want to take full advantage of its natural sweetness, it can be cooked, but it is better raw, and makes excellent juice.

Golden Delicious [2]

Firm, sweet, juicy, crunchy, aromas of vanilla (when well grown). Multipurpose, but best for baking.

This classic apple that originated in West Virginia, US, is the one most widely found on commercial circuits. Golden Delicious apples are a supermarket mainstay in most of the world, but the question is: does this variety deserve its success? The best Golden Delicious are grown at medium altitudes, and these are the only apples in France that have a PDO (Protected Designation of Origin) status. At their worst, when intensively farmed, they are watery and bland, the sort of thing one would expect to find in a school cafeteria. Yet it is also the apple most widely used by French pastry chefs, because if its flesh, which holds when cooked. So let's focus on the finer Golden Delicious, those PDO from the Limousin and Savoie regions, that are allowed to ripen until their pale yellow skin flushes pink, and whose sweet, vanilla taste is the best the variety can offer. They come into season in September, but it goes without saying that intensively farmed Golden Delicious are available year-round.

Granny Smith [6]

Firm, very tart, juicy, holds well when cooked. A cooking apple that is also good as a dessert apple, but under certain conditions.

This apple was developed in Australia by a certain Mrs. Maria Ana Smith in 1868. It arrived in the US in the late 1960s, and is one of the most well known apple varieties. With its smooth green color (the ultimate apple green), its waxy skin, and characteristic oblong shape, it is always recognizable. However, the color is not entirely natural: the apple is harvested around September, before it is completely ripe (hence its acidity). If it ripens fully on the tree, it turns a yellowy pink and its flavors become more pronounced. Alongside the Golden Delicious, and because it holds so well when cooked, it is a favorite among pastry chefs, who tend to use the one for its sweetness and the other for its sourness. It is also widely used raw in savory recipes, particularly because its flesh browns more slowly than that of the other varieties. However, because it is not quite ripe, it is best to avoid biting into it raw.

Jonagold and Jonagored [5]

Softens nicely when cooked, crisp when raw, sweet, juicy, and fragrant. Perfect for tarts, desserts, and applesauce.

The Jonagold is a hybrid of the Golden Delicious and the Jonathan, a classic American variety. It was created in 1943 in New York State. It is good both raw and cooked, with its flesh softening nicely when cooked. The Jonagored is a sport (a natural genetic mutation) of the Jonagold.

Juliet

Firm, crisp, juicy, fragrant (with notes of rose). Good sweet-sour balance. A dessert and cooking apple, usually organic.

This delicious apple was developed in France using exclusively organic growing practices–one of the first in the world–and was re-created in the US by three universities. It is gaining in popularity and is increasingly exported from France. It is a lovely bright red color on a yellow background, and it is firm and shiny, with fine-tasting, crisp white flesh that has just the right degree of firmness. We advise it for all uses, but particularly for juice, unpeeled. (Since it's organic, that does not pose a problem; just don't forget to wash it.)

Pink Lady® [3]
(Variety name: Cripps' Pink)

Firm, sweet, juicy. A dessert apple and one for juice.

Crisp with an attractive pinky color, the Pink Lady, developed in Australia from the Golden Delicious and Lady Williams, is easy to find. It is the only truly pink apple. But intensive production worsens its less desirable tendencies and those you find in supermarkets are often watery and bland. This sort of farming uses massive amounts of pesticides, so it's best to hunt out organic Pink Lady® apples. It is not really suitable for cooking or for baking.

King of the Pippins
(Reine des Reinettes)

Firm, crisp, fragrant, sweet, juicy, truly excellent raw and cooked. A good apple for tarts, upside-down apple tarts (tarte Tatin) in particular.

The Reinette family includes more than one hundred varieties. It originated in France and dates back to the 1770s. The apples are medium-sized fruits that do not really fit a single description. Any round, slightly flattened apple whose eye is smooth and free of bumps is considered to be Reinette-shaped, unlike the Calville shapes (see Calville), which are bumpy, asymmetrical, and have ribbing around the eye. The Reinettes vary greatly in terms of taste and texture. The Reine des Reinettes is a matte yellow striated with orange and

red. Its delicate, delicious flavor evokes fresh walnuts (and in fact we like to eat it raw, accompanied by walnuts). It is one of the finest apples for baking and pastry.

Reinette Clochard

Firm, crunchy, juicy, sweet, fragrant with vanilla notes; keeps well, good sliced, also excellent for pastry making.

This small heirloom Reinette of a variety that was almost forgotten made its comeback in France some fifteen years ago, and is now a star. The name translates to "homeless" or "tramp little queen"–with reinette meaning "little queen." It originated in the west of France, in the Charente, Poitou, and Vendée regions, where it is still widely found. Because it traveled well, it was the first apple exported from France. Yellow and round, sometimes with an orange blush on one side, it is covered in minute black spots. A late apple, it can be eaten right through winter, and keeps until well into spring. Its sweet vanilla flavor is reminiscent of that of the Chantecler–not surprising, because the Chantecler was bred from the Clochard and the Golden Delicious. It is also comparable to the McIntosh, an old North American variety.

Reinette Grise du Canada [9]
Also known as Pomme Gris and Pomme Grise

Very firm, little juice, very sour, good for cooking and for tarts.

This is a grey, greenish, rough, lightly flattened apple. Its flesh is compact, white, firm, and tangy, and so it is excellent when paired with savory dishes. (In France, it is the apple traditionally served with boudin aux pommes–blood sausage with apples.) Because it can reach sizable proportions, it also bears the moniker of *monstrueuse* du Canada (gigantic one of Canada), when in reality it originated in England. It has a good texture for pastry-making, but do check on just how sour it is so you can adjust the sweetening.

Tentation® [4]
Also known as Delblush.

Firm, sweet, juicy, crunchy, delicately tangy, excellent for pastry-making and for candied confections.

Created in 1979 by the Delbard orchards in France, the Tentation® is a cross between the Golden Delicious and a variety called the Blushing Golden. It has obvious similarities to the Golden Delicious, but with a little more sourness. The shape is oblong (it is taller than it is wide) and the color is pale yellow with a pink blush. The Tentation® has notes of sugarcane, aniseed, and quince, with just a hint of mint. It is excellent for tarts and upside-down cakes, and poached in vanilla-scented syrup.

Akane

Tokyo Rose

**Firm, juicy, sour, aromatic, early season.
Mainly to be eaten sliced and juiced.**

This attractive little apple comes to us from Japan (it is also known as the Tokyo Rose). It can be found at markets in mid-August–the first apple to appear–but the season does not last long, for it is rarely available after October. The skin is a lovely, intense red over pale yellow that verges on white. The flesh is white, crunchy, juicy, tangy, and transparent, with a slight taste of strawberry. If cooked, it becomes very fragile; it is best eaten sliced or juiced.

Idared

**Tender, juicy, mild-tasting, aromatic, and rather tangy. Good
eaten out of hand and to cook for applesauce.**

Developed in the 1930s in Idaho, this attractive, large-sized red apple appears in fall. Its crisp but delicate white flesh softens when cooked, so it is perfect for applesauce and marmalades. It is also excellent eaten raw. The Idared grown in climates with cold winters can be extraordinary, with a heady fragrance and aroma.

Junami

**Very firm, juicy, crisp, with a good sweet-sour balance.
A good apple to bite into.**

The lovely red of this Swiss-developed apple is due to the fact that it is a hybrid of the Elstar, Maigold, and Idared varieties. It is crisp, refreshing, and richly flavored. We prefer to eat it raw.

Melrose

**Very firm and crisp, fragrant, with a good sweet-sour
balance. An apple to slice, as well as for baking, juicing,
and making hard cider.**

This is the official apple of Ohio State. It is notable for its attractive red color and may grow to a considerable size. It is harvested late and is a good winter apple. The Melrose is suitable for both pastry-making and eating raw.

Rubinette

**Very firm, crisp, aromatic, with a good sweet-sharp balance.
An apple to enjoy raw and to cook, excellent in jams.**

A cross between the Cox's Orange Pippin and the Golden Delicious, the Rubinette was developed in Switzerland in 1964. In Europe, it flourishes in eastern France, Switzerland, and Germany, and it grows in orchards in Northern America. Orange or green, and striated with red, it is a versatile apple. It is renowned for its delicacy and flavor and is a favorite in family orchards in France. Because it retains its crunchiness and good texture even when cooked, it is perfect for jams and chutneys.

Anisa
(Pomme d'Anis)

Very firm and very juicy, crisp, tangy, and with an aroma of aniseed. An apple to eat out of hand, cook with, and for hard cider.

Small, round, and rough-skinned, this bronze apple with a fiery red blush is an attractive variety found in the southwest of France, in the Basque region in particular, where it bears the name of Anisa and where it is a favorite for hard ciders and artisanal juice. With its extremely firm flesh, it is an excellent apple to slice and to use in tarts. If you are in the southwest of France in fall, look out for it at farmers' markets.

Blenheim Orange Apple [15]
(Bénédictin, Bénédictin de Jumiège, Reinette Normande)

Of average firmness, but flavorful with a good sweet-sour balance. White, mild flesh. Versatile, good for hard cider.

This very old heirloom variety is harvested in fall. In France, the monks at Jumièges Abbey in Normandy used to grow it; today it grows mainly in Haute-Normandie. Of average size and round, it is good for all purposes, including for making cider (and hence for juice). It softens nicely when cooked but retains its shape, making it ideal for the tarte Tatin (apple-upside-down cake).

Calville

Firm, aromatic, crisp, juicy, sour–an excellent multipurpose apple.

In France, the name Calville, like that of Reinette, refers not to one apple but to a group of very old heirloom varieties that are ribbed, asymmetrical, elongated to various degrees, often lopsided, and often ribbed around the eye with waxy skin. They are firm, juicy, and versatile, rich in vitamins and very flavorful. At farmers' markets in the French countryside, various types of Calville can be found, including the Calville Blanche, Calville Rouge, Lombarts Calville, and Calville du Roi. They ripen either in fall or in winter, depending on the type. The winter Calville Blanche was said to be the favorite apple of Louis XIV; trees were planted at orchards of Versailles. It is depicted in Renaissance paintings and in one of Monet's still lifes.

Guillevic

Juicy, sweet, delicate, fragrant–one of the best apples for hard cider. Can also be eaten raw.

This is not an apple you'll find easily at farmers' markets in France, and even less at supermarkets. But this yellow variety that comes from the Morbihan, part of Brittany, is one of the best hard cider apples there is. It gives plentiful juice that is clear and sweet, making for a remarkably fine monovarietal hard cider. If you're hunting for some of the best French hard ciders, look out for "Pur Guillevic" or "100% Guillevic" on the labels.

Lady Apple
(Api)

"Pomme de reinette et pomme d'api..."

All French children learn a nursery rhyme that starts with the name of two apples, Pomme de Reinette and Pomme d'Api. Although many have probably eaten a Reinette, it is doubtful whether any have actually tasted an Api (the more common name in Europe), an old French variety that is now very rare. It is thought to have been discovered in Brittany, in the Forest of Api, and dates back to the sixteenth century. Small, flattened, and slightly lop-sided, the Lady apple is often pale green or yellow with a bright red cheek; there is also a larger cultivar, the Api Noir, or Black Lady apple. Should you stumble upon a country market where they are on sale, don't hesitate to try them: they are delicate, crisp, refreshing, and full of flavor–the perfect apple to eat out of hand.

Patte-de-Loup [14]

Very firm, crisp, sour, fragrant, of average juiciness. Excellent for pastry-making.

This apple is immediately recognizable thanks to the long, deep scar on one side of the fruit, as if it had been scratched by a wolf–its name means "wolf's paw." This small round, grey-green, rough-skinned apple is a very old variety thought to date back to at least the Middle Ages; it originated in the Maine-et-Loire part of the Loire region. It is going through a revival in France, particularly with organic farmers, and can now be found at farmers' markets. We are fond of this rustic late-season apple, sold through winter and in spring, for its tangy taste with hints of aniseed. It's one of the finest apples there is.

Rambo
(Rambour)
Softens when cooked, tender when raw, tangy. A good cooking apple.

Very many varieties of heirloom apples bear the name of Rambos (there are winter and summer Rambos, for example), first recorded in France in 1535 and once widely grown in parts of the US. They are large and slightly flattened, irregularly shaped. The flesh is soft and they are better cooked than raw–in fact, they are perfect for applesauce. With their tartness, they are excellent paired with savory dishes, such as game and roasts.

Reinette d'Armorique [13]
Firm, crisp, sweet, fragrant, with a good sweet-sour balance. A versatile apple good for slicing, pastry-making, juice, and hard cider.

Armorique is part of the Brittany region and this apple also bears the name of Reinette de Bretagne. It is harvested in the fall and keeps for a very long time. Yellow with a red blush, the skin is scabbed with rough, grey marbling. It is highly appreciated in its growing region, a peninsula, where it is still widely grown. A fine multipurpose apple in all respects.

Reinette de Bauilleul [12]
Firm, juicy, crisp, fragrant. An apple to cook and to eat out of hand. Use for hard cider, jelly, and to make sucres de pomme, a confection made in Normandy.

This traditional round, slightly flattened apple is green with red striations. No one knows why it also bears the name of Gros Hôpital (big hospital), but it can grow to a large size. The shiny, waxy skin hides a very dense flesh, making this a weighty fruit. In fact, a local saying in Normandy, where it originates, makes an offensive allusion to its weight. If you are traveling in Haute-Normandie or in Picardy, you will find it at farmers' markets. There is nothing you can't do with the Bailleul: slice it, make tarts and applesauce, but mainly hard cider and jellies–it is rich in pectin.

Rouget de Dol
Very firm, crisp. It keeps well and is very versatile, particularly good for hard cider.

The Rouget de Dol, a small red apple, is one of the classic varieties of the Ile-et-Vilaine area. Much appreciated as an apple for hard cider, it is versatile and good both raw and cooked.

Sartha's Yellow
(Reinette du Mans, Reinette Jaune)
Firm when harvested, tender when ripe. Fleshy with a slight tang and a vanilla fragrance. Cooking and eating apple.

The Reinette du Mans comes from the area around Le Mans, in the Sarthe region. It was developed early in the nineteenth century. It is rather large, and a light green-yellow (jaune means "yellow") dotted with small grey spots. It is highly recommended for tarte Tatin, because its flesh softens even though it retains its shape. It is also an excellent apple for applesauce.

Wise Apple
(Court Pendu)
Firm, very fragrant, crisp, sweet. A dessert apple, for pastry and hard cider.

Court Pendu Rouge, Blanc, Plat, and Dur…This is a particularly old French variety of apple, with references going back to at least 1613; it was popular in Victorian times as a dessert apple. They are large-sized apples with delicate white flesh, very flavorful and sweet, and a distinctive, slightly sour, aniseed-like aftertaste. In the past they were thought to have medicinal virtues; they enjoyed the reputation of being the best of all apples.

Yellow Bellflower
(Belle-Fleur or Belle-Fleur Jaune)
Firm, juicy, sweet. Versatile, an excellent dessert apple.

This apple originated in New Jersey, and can be dated back to 1742. Fairly large and oblong, it is very attractive, with a bright yellow skin and an orange-hued blush on one side. Yellow Bellflowers are often lopsided, with a smooth skin, sometimes speckled with small black spots. The flesh is firm, crisp, and sweet, somewhat reminiscent of that of the Golden Delicious, although it has more character.

Yellow Transparent
(Transparente de Croncels)
Softens well when cooked, juicy, not crunchy, slightly tart. Mainly a culinary apple.

This large-sized apple, not to be confused with the other Transparents, owes its name to its skin–pale yellow with a red blush–that gives an impression of transparency. It is one of the early apples (August and September), and must not be harvested when too ripe, or it will be mealy. In fact, it is best eaten slightly under-ripe. If you are looking for an apple that softens well when cooked, this one is perfect. In fact, it is best cooked.

19
Crunchy

43
Crisp

79
Soft

Crunchy

We like to make these tartlets with red apples, which give a pretty floral effect. However, if you use several varieties, you will create a bouquet of different-colored roses: red, yellow, orange, and even pale green.

Apple Roses

MAKES 10 ROSES
(IN TEN 3-INCH/8-CM SILICONE MOLDS)

4 large apples of different colors
Juice of 1 lemon
1 lb. (500 g) puff pastry (see page 58), or store-bought
1 egg, lightly beaten, for the egg wash
7¾ oz. (220 g) applesauce, about 1 scant cup (see page 29)
7 tablespoons (3½ oz. / 100 g) butter, melted until lukewarm
5 ounces (150 g) quince jelly for the glaze

Core the apples, but of course, do not peel them. Cut them in half from top to bottom.

Have a bowl of cold water ready with the lemon juice stirred in.

Using a mandoline, slice the apples very thinly, dipping them immediately in the bowl of water so that they do not brown.

Place the bowl with the apple slices in the microwave oven on medium-high (600W) for 1 minute to soften them slightly. If you do not have a microwave oven, simply warm the lemony water and leave the slices until slightly softened.

Drain the slices and pat them dry carefully. Sort them according to the color of their skins.

Preheat the oven to 350°F (180°C).

Roll the puff pastry into a 16 by 25-inch (40 by 60-cm) rectangle and brush it with the egg wash. Cut the rectangle into ten strips, each 2½ inches (6 cm) and 16 inches (40 cm) long. Using one color of apple per rose tartlet, place the apple slices along the strip of puff pastry, overlapping them like roof tiles. Leave just under ½ inch (1 cm) overhang of apple–skin side on the exterior–on one side of the pastry strip. In the center of the apple slices, drizzle a line of applesauce from one end to the other.

Fold the strip into two, pressing down lightly on the end, and then roll it up in a spiral. Place each rose in a silicone mold with the visible part of the apples facing upward, and brush generously with the melted butter.

Bake for 40 to 45 minutes, checking regularly on how they are coloring. Remove them when the pastry is a lovely golden color. Immediately turn the roses out of the molds and allow to cool on a rack.

Lightly heat the quince jelly and luster the roses with it to give them a nice sheen.

If you are lucky enough to have an apple orchard, or access to a farmers' market, and can find very small apples, this is a recipe for you.

Mini Candy Apples

SERVES 6

18 very small apples of similar size
6 licorice root sticks
2⅔ cups (1 lb. 2 oz. / 500 g) sugar
6 tablespoons mineral water
2 teaspoons lemon juice
A few drops of red food coloring

Wash the apples and dry them thoroughly. Skewer three apples on each of the licorice sticks and set aside.

Pour some very cold water into the sink or a large pot—you will need this to stop the caramel cooking any further when it has reached the right temperature.

Pour the sugar into a heavy-bottomed saucepan and stir in the mineral water, lemon juice, and food coloring. Cook over low heat without stirring, until the syrup forms an amber-colored caramel. If you have an instant-read thermometer, it should register about 345°F (175°C). Immediately remove from the heat and place the saucepan in the sink so that the bottom is in direct contact with the cold water.

Dip the apples in the liquid caramel, remove them, and place them to dry on a sheet of parchment or wax paper protected from moisture.

n the region of Haute-Normandie, this dessert was traditionally prepared just before the meal so that the fruit would have time to macerate. It was accompanied by cookies and boudoir biscuits (ladyfingers), and guests would drink up the sweetened wine directly from their bowl when they'd finished the fruit. No spices are added: the wine and fruit are sufficiently tasty. In the past, the apple cores were not removed with a cookie cutter as we do here. The apples selected were firm and sweet. We recommend Royal Gala, Chantecler, Pippins, or Golden Delicious.

Apple and Orange Salad

IN RED WINE

SERVES 4

4 medium apples or 2 large ones
1 large orange or 2 small ones, unwaxed or organic
½ cup (2 oz. / 50 g) light brown sugar or granulated sugar
1 bottle red wine

Wash and dry the fruit. Remove the stalk and base of the apples, and peel them, keeping them whole. Slice the apples and unpeeled orange into round ⅛-inch (3 to 4 mm) slices. Arrange them in a large bowl, alternating apple and orange slices, and lightly dusting each layer with sugar.

Pour the wine over the fruit, cover the serving bowl, and allow to macerate at room temperature for 1 hour.

Serve, placing the slices upright if you prefer, in bowls or soup plates, accompanied by cookies of your choice.

When strawberries, mangoes, melons, and more are in season, add them to the salad, cut into small cubes. The varieties of apple we give here are suggestions only: choose from whatever takes your fancy among the seasonal apples, trying to contrast the tastes. Most importantly, serve this tartare as soon as possible after you have prepared it. The apple juice, however, should be made ahead: leave time for it to chill well so that it is cold when you pour it over the tartare.

Apple Tartare

SERVES 4 TO 6

APPLE JUICE
(make ahead)
¾ cup (200 ml) apple stock (see page 174)
¼ cup (50 ml) hard apple cider
Juice of ½ lemon

TARTARE
1 Granny Smith apple
1 Golden Delicious apple
1 Pink Lady® or Fuji apple
1 Victoria pineapple or ½ a pineapple of one of the more common varieties
1 kiwi
Juice of ½ lemon
Finely grated zest of 1 or 2 limes
A few basil leaves (or small edible flowers)

To make the juice, pour the apple stock, hard cider, and lemon juice into a saucepan and place over medium-low heat. Cook slowly until reduced to a thick liquid. Allow to cool and chill well in the refrigerator.

Wash and dry the apples, leaving the skin on. Peel the pineapple and kiwi. Cut all of the fruit into very small cubes (this is known as a *brunoise*).

Place all the cubed fruit in a serving dish and drizzle the lemon juice over. Stir to combine and pour over the apple juice.

Just before serving, scatter the lime zest over the tartare and garnish with the basil leaves or flowers.

édric Grolet, pastry chef at the luxury Hôtel Meurice in Paris, is the creator of this refined, delicate tart, made—unusually—with almost-raw apple slices. He has generously shared his recipe with us. Do make the sweet buttery pastry a day ahead. If you don't have a tart ring (these are best for baking the crust), simply use a tart pan with a removable bottom.

Apple Tart

BY CÉDRIC GROLET

MAKES ONE 10-INCH (24 CM) TART FOR 8

SWEET PASTRY

1 stick plus 2 tablespoons (5¼ oz. / 150 g) butter, at a warm room temperature
¾ cup (3¼ oz. / 95 g) confectioners' sugar
Generous ⅓ cup (1 oz. / 30 g) almond flour
¼ teaspoon (1 g) Guérande salt, or other coarsely ground sea salt
Heaping ¼ teaspoon (1 g) ground vanilla (or ½ teaspoon vanilla extract)
1 extra-large egg (2 oz. / 60 g, the equivalent of ¼ cup lightly beaten egg)
2 cups (9 oz. / 250 g) all-purpose flour

ALMOND CREAM

1 stick plus 2 tablespoons (5¼ oz. / 150 g) butter, at a warm room temperature
¾ cup (5¼ oz. / 150 g) sugar
1½ cup (5¼ oz. / 150 g) almond flour
3 large eggs (5¼ oz. / 150 g, the equivalent of ⅔ cup)

APPLESAUCE

4 Granny Smith apples
½ cup (125 g) lemon juice

APPLE TOPPING

4 Royal Gala apples
7 tablespoons (3½ oz. / 100 g) butter, plus extra for the pan

28

CRUNCHY

FOR THE SWEET PASTRY (MAKE A DAY AHEAD)

In the bowl of a stand mixer fitted with the paddle attachment, combine the butter, confectioners' sugar, almond flour, salt, and ground vanilla. When creamed, add the lightly beaten egg and beat until the mixture forms an emulsion. Then, working at low speed, gradually add the flour, stopping just when it is thoroughly incorporated. Shape the dough into a ball, flatten it into a disk, cover in plastic wrap, and place in the refrigerator to chill.

FOR THE ALMOND CREAM

In the bowl of the stand mixer fitted with the paddle attachment, cream the butter, sugar, and almond flour together. Add the eggs, one by one. Transfer the almond cream into a pastry bag fitted with a wide plain tip, ensure that none of it will run out, and place in the refrigerator.

FOR THE APPLESAUCE

Peel and core the Granny Smith apples and cut them into small cubes. Combine the apple cubes and lemon juice in a saucepan and cook over medium heat, stirring from time to time. When the apples have softened considerably–there should still be pieces visible–remove from the heat. Allow to cool slightly, cover the applesauce with plastic wrap, and place in the refrigerator.

ASSEMBLE, MAKE APPLE TOPPING, AND BAKE THE TART

Remove the sweet pastry from the refrigerator a few minutes before rolling it out. Butter the sides of the tart ring (as well as the bottom, if you are using a tart pan). Roll the dough to a thickness of ⅛ inch (3 mm). Set the tart ring over a baking sheet lined with parchment or baking paper and snugly fit the dough into it. Place in the refrigerator for about 30 minutes.

Preheat the oven to 375°F (190°C). Pipe the almond cream over the tart crust, filling it half-way to the top of the rim. Place in the oven and immediately reduce the temperature to 340°F (170°C). Bake for 25 to 30 minutes, until the almond cream is lightly browned. Allow to cool. For the next step, you will need the oven at 350°F (180°C).

With an offset spatula, spread the applesauce over the baked almond cream very thinly (the layer should be about ⅛ inch / 3 mm thick).

In a small saucepan, melt the butter. Continue cooking until it has browned. This is called *beurre noisette*, hazelnut butter. Strain it through a fine-mesh sieve.

Wash the Royal Gala apples and core them with an apple corer. Using a mandoline with safety guard (or electric slicer), slice them thinly. Cut each slice in half and, starting at the rim, arrange the slices in a rose pattern, pressing the outward slices lightly against the crust (see photo on following page).

Brush the browned butter over the apples and return the tart to the oven for 10 minutes. Serve warm.

Trompe l'Oeil Apple "Ice Cubes"

MAKES ABOUT 40 "ICE CUBES"

¾ cup (200 ml) hard, dry apple cider
¾ cup (200 ml) apple juice
½ cup (3½ oz. / 100 g) sugar
1 teaspoon (0.7 oz. / 2 g) agar agar powder
(make sure that this is a level teaspoon, and no more)

SPECIAL EQUIPMENT
Disposable ice cube bags

In a saucepan, begin heating the cider and apple juice.
Combine the sugar and agar agar.
As soon as the liquid comes to a boil, pour in the dry ingredients.
Stir well and bring back to a rolling boil for 3 minutes. Transfer to a bowl or jug.
Allow to cool, checking the temperature with a thermometer. When the mixture has cooled to 105°F (40°C), carefully pour it into the ice cube bags.
Place in the refrigerator for at least 2 hours, then carefully cut the bags open to release the "ice cubes".

These softened apple slices are arranged on a plate like a carpaccio. It's essential to select a variety of apple that holds up well when cooked, so go for King of the Pippins, Rubinette, Belle de Boskoop, or Golden Delicious. Keep in mind that the Pippins are more transparent when cooked. Prepare the apples at least twelve hours ahead so that your salad will be well chilled when you serve it.

Poached Apple Salad

SERVES 4

¾ cup (200 ml) apple stock (see page 174) or water
1 cup (7 oz. / 200 g) sugar
1 stick cinnamon
1 vanilla bean, split lengthwise and seeds scraped
4 apples
A few raspberries, cut into halves
Black sesame seeds for sprinkling
Small edible flowers
Dash of olive oil

Make a syrup: In a large saucepan or a pot, bring the apple stock and sugar to a boil with the cinnamon stick and the vanilla bean and seeds. Wash and peel the apples. Using a mandoline with safety guard (or electric slicer), slice them finely. Add them to the syrup and bring back to a boil.

Immediately remove from the heat and cover the saucepan with the lid. Ensure that the temperature remains at 175°F (80°C) for 25 minutes; using an instant-read thermometer, check the temperature of the apples as they soak in the syrup. If the temperature drops below 175°F (80°C), re-heat gently.

Then allow to cool and place in the refrigerator to chill for 12 hours (or overnight).

To serve, arrange the apple slices around individual plates and pour over just enough syrup to cover them. Dot with the raspberries, sprinkle with the black sesame seeds, and scatter the edible flowers over the top. Drizzle with a little olive oil just before serving.

Here we use two varieties of apple to vary the textures and tastes. The trusty Granny Smith is included for its acidity and the Pink Lady, for its natural sweetness. One couldn't wish for more in terms of firm texture and crispness, both of which make this refreshing salad even more appetizing. The syrup for the salad dressing can be made ahead and stored in the refrigerator.

Refreshing Apple Salad

WITH VANILLA-SCENTED OLIVE OIL SALAD DRESSING

SERVES 4

VANILLA-SCENTED OLIVE OIL SALAD DRESSING
2 vanilla beans
Scant ½ cup (100 ml) water
½ cup (3½ oz. / 100 g) sugar
Scant ¼ cup (50 ml) extra virgin olive oil
Juice of 2 limes

SALAD
2 slices brioche (or challah)
2 tablespoons extra virgin olive oil
4 Granny Smith apples
4 Pink Lady apples
1 lime
1 bunch mint
Edible pansies

FOR THE VANILLA-SCENTED OLIVE OIL SALAD DRESSING

Split the vanilla beans in two lengthwise and scrape out the seeds. Combine the water and sugar in a saucepan. Place over low heat with the vanilla beans and seeds. When the sugar has dissolved, bring to a boil. Remove from the heat, cover with the lid, and allow to cool. Strain the cooled syrup through a fine-mesh sieve into a bowl and whisk in the olive oil and lime juice. Reserve in the refrigerator.

FOR THE SALAD

Preheat the oven to 350°F (180°C).
Cut the brioche slices into small cubes and roll them in the olive oil to coat. Place them on a baking sheet lined with parchment or baking paper and bake for 12 minutes, turning them over from time to time, until golden. Transfer to a rack and allow to cool.
Wash the apples but do not peel them. Using a mandoline with safety guard (or electric slicer), slice them finely. Immediately coat them with the lime juice so that they do not brown.

TO PLATE

Arrange the apple slices attractively in soup plates or bowls. Drizzle with the salad dressing and dot the brioche croutons over the top. Scatter with small mint leaves and a few edible pansies.

Apple-Pecan Chocolate Bar

MAKES 10 BARS

APPLES
5 large apples
5 tablespoons (3 oz. / 80 g) salted butter
3½ tablespoons (2½ oz. / 75 g) multi-floral honey

CARAMELIZED PECANS
5½ oz. (160 g) shelled, unsalted pecans (about 1⅓ cups)
⅔ cup (3 oz. / 80 g) confectioners' sugar

ASSEMBLY
1½ lb. (700 g) milk chocolate, chopped (or wafers)

SPECIAL EQUIPMENT
2 food-grade metallic ruler bars, each 39 inches (1 m) long and ¼ inch (7 mm) thick
2 food-grade metallic ruler bars, each 4 inches (10 cm) long and ¼ inch (7 mm) thick
or
An adjustable rectangular cake frame
1 metal brush
or
A fine icing comb

These chocolate bars are crunchy, thanks to the caramelized pecans, and have a pronounced tart note, thanks to the apples. If you don't have food-grade ruler bars, simply pour the chocolate into small rectangular dishes lined with wax paper. Alternatively, you can use an adjustable rectangular cake frame.

FOR THE APPLES

Peel and core the apples. Cut them into a very small dice, with sides of about ⅛ inch (3 mm). (Dice of this size is known as a *salpicon*.) Melt the butter in a skillet over medium heat. As soon as it sizzles, add the diced apples. Cook, stirring from time to time, until translucent. Carefully stir in the honey and bring to a boil. Boil for 1 minute, then transfer to a mixing bowl.

FOR THE CARAMELIZED PECANS

Chop the pecans. Sift the confectioners' sugar. In a saucepan, combine the pecans with the confectioners' sugar. Cook over medium heat, stirring constantly, until the nuts are coated in caramel. Pour them directly onto a sheet of wax paper, spreading them gently with a spatula to make an even layer. When they are cool enough to handle, separate those that are stuck together.

ASSEMBLE THE CHOCOLATE BARS

Dampen the work surface with water. Spread plastic wrap over it, flattening it well to eliminate as many folds as possible. If you are using ruler bars, place them at a distance of 4 inches (10 cm). Place the shorter bars at each end, so that you have a rectangular frame. Arrange the apple dice evenly over the surface of the rectangle.

Over a hot water bath or in the microwave oven, heat two-thirds of the chocolate to 113°F (45°C). Stir until smooth and then add the remaining chocolate. Stir to slightly melt this chocolate, then process briefly with an immersion blender, stopping when it is completely smooth. Stir in the caramelized pecans and pour the chocolate into the rectangular frame, covering the diced apple. Allow to firm up completely, then brush the tablet along the length with the metal brush to create a stripy effect.

Slide a knife between the metal ruler bars and the chocolate so that you can remove the rulers. Cut the chocolate into 4-inch (10-cm) squares and store, well wrapped, in the refrigerator.

A French chocolate confection, based on a dish of raisins, dried figs, and nuts, which these days are studded on chocolate disks, mendiants take their name from the four monastic mendicant orders of the Roman Catholic church. The colors of the fruit and nuts represented the Dominicans, Augustinians, Carmelites, and Franciscans, who all lived on charitable offerings, hence their name of *mendiants*, which means "beggars." Mendiants are often given at Christmas. In our take, the disks are made of chocolate-coated apple chips.

Apple Mendiants

MAKES 20 MENDIANTS

35 whole, peeled hazelnuts
1 lb. 10 oz. (750 g) bittersweet chocolate, chopped or in wafers
¾ teaspoon (2 g) ground vanilla bean
½ teaspoon (3 g) vanilla extract
Heaping ¼ teaspoon (2 g) fine sea salt
1 teaspoon (5 g) edible shiny bronze powder
20 apple chips (see page 48)

Spread the hazelnuts on a baking sheet and place in a 340°F (170°C) oven for about 20 minutes, until nicely colored inside. Keep an eye on them as they roast so that they do not burn. Allow to cool.

Over a hot water bath or in the microwave oven, heat two-thirds of the chocolate to 113°F (45°C). Stir until smooth and then stir in the remaining chocolate. Stir to slightly melt this chocolate, then allow to melt completely (this should take a few moments). Stir in the ground vanilla bean, vanilla extract, and salt. Process briefly with an immersion blender, stopping when it is completely smooth.

Holding the hazelnuts on a dipping fork, dip them completely into the melted chocolate. Place on a sheet of wax paper and then in the refrigerator to chill for 5 minutes. Then coat them in the shiny powder and cut them into halves.

Arrange the apple chips on a rack and smooth the chocolate over each one. Lightly rap the rack so that any excess chocolate drips off.

On each mendiant, place 3 hazelnut halves (see photo on facing page). Allow the disks to firm up completely, then store them in an airtight container.

Crisp

A ny firm, slightly tangy apple is suitable for this simple dessert. The Pippins are particularly recommended. Fry these fritters until they are very well colored: they should almost be overdone.

Apple Fritters

SERVES 4 TO 6

4 eggs
3 tablespoons (2 oz. / 50 g) butter
2 cups (9 oz. / 250 g) all-purpose flour, sifted
1 heaping tablespoon (15 g) sugar, plus a pinch for the egg whites
1 teaspoon (5 g) salt
Scant ½ cup (100 ml) milk
⅔ cup (150 ml) blond ale
4 Pippin apples
Oil for frying (a neutral oil such as grapeseed oil, sunflower oil, or Canola oil)

Separate the eggs. Melt the butter and allow it to cool to lukewarm, but do not allow it to set.

In the bowl of a stand mixer fitted with the paddle attachment, combine the flour, sugar, and salt. Beat in the milk and the egg yolks. When combined, replace the paddle attachment with the whisk and pour in the beer. Whisk until light and airy, and thoroughly combined.

Strain the batter through a fine-mesh sieve into a bowl. Stir in the melted butter and allow to rest for 30 minutes.

Whisk the egg whites with a pinch of sugar to the soft peak stage. Using a flexible spatula, fold them carefully into the batter.

Peel the apples and cut them into thick slices.

Heat the oil to 340°F (170°C).

Holding the apple pieces on the tines of a fork, dip them into the batter to coat.

Working in batches, drop them carefully into the hot oil and fry for about 9 minutes.

Drain the fritters on two layers of paper towels and serve hot.

A surprising recipe that you should prepare so that it is also aesthetically pleasing: use several types of apples of varying colors–include red, yellow, orange, green, and even grey. Wash them and pat them dry very carefully, using paper towels, then use a vegetable peeler to make long strips. Ensure that not a single drop of water remains on the peel! You can use the flesh as you please. Make sure that the batter is very cold (that's why ice cubes are included in the ingredients list), and the oil, very hot. This guarantees a temperature shock that makes for the best tempura.

Apple Peel Tempura

SERVES 4

Peel of 8 apples of different varieties
4 cups (1 liter) oil for frying
(a neutral oil such as grapeseed oil, sunflower oil, or Canola oil)
1⅔ cups (7 oz. / 200 g) all-purpose flour
⅔ cup (3½ oz. / 100 g) potato starch
1 pinch salt
1⅔ cups (400 ml) hard apple cider, chilled
10 to 12 ice cubes
Sugar for sprinkling (optional)

Wash and dry the apples very carefully. Set them aside.
Sift the flour, potato starch, and salt together in a mixing bowl. Make a well in the center and gradually pour in the hard cider, stirring constantly so that no lumps form. Add the ice cubes.
In a very large pot or fryer, heat the oil to 400°F (200°C).
While the oil is heating, use a vegetable peeler to cut the apple skins into long strips.
Prepare a dish lined with plenty of paper towels.
When the oil has come to temperature, use chopsticks or tongs to dip the strips of peel into the batter, coating them completely. Working in batches if necessary, carefully drop them directly into the oil. Remove them when they are nicely golden and place on the paper towels to drain.
Serve warm, sprinkled with sugar if you wish.

To make these chips, use firm-fleshed apples that do not soften easily, such as Golden Delicious, Granny Smith, Chantecler, Belle de Boskoop (which has more tang), Rubinette, or any of the Pippins.

Apple Chips

SERVES 8

1⅔ cups (400 ml) water
½ cup (3½ oz. / 100 g) sugar
3½ oz. (100 g) isomalt
4 apples

Make a syrup: Bring the water with the sugar and isomalt to a boil. Pour it into a large shallow baking dish or rimmed baking sheet.

Wash the apples and, using a mandoline or electric slicer, cut them into very thin slices widthwise.

Immediately drop them into the hot syrup and allow to macerate at room temperature for about 5 hours.

Preheat the oven to 210°F (100°C).

Drain the apple slices on sheets of paper towel and arrange them on baking sheets lined with silicone baking mats.

Place in the oven for about 1 hour, until completely dried. When cooled, store in an airtight container.

A contraction of *barquette* (small boat) and *tartelette* (tartlet), the barlette is an éclair-shaped tartlet. For this recipe, I recommend using Golden Delicious apples, but of course you can also use other firm, sweet varieties, such as Pippins, Jonagold, Chantecler, Royal Gala, and Reinette Clochard. If you would like your barlettes to have greater crispness and sharpness, use Granny Smith, Juliet, Rubinette, or Belle de Boskoop apples. Note that this recipe requires an accurate scale to make the olive oil and vanilla ganache.

Apple Barlette

MAKES 10 PASTRIES

SWEET HAZELNUT PASTE

Scant ⅔ cup (3 oz. / 90 g)
all-purpose flour

¼ teaspoon (1 g) fine sea salt

Scant ⅓ cup (1½ oz. / 40 g)
confectioners' sugar

¼ teaspoon (1 g) ground vanilla

2½ tablespoons (15 g)
ground hazelnuts

2½ tablespoons (1 oz. /
25 g) potato starch

4 tablespoons (2 oz. / 60 g)
butter, in small cubes

1 tablespoon plus 1 teaspoon
(20 g) egg, lightly beaten

CARAMELIZED PISTACHIOS

5½ oz. (155 g) peeled, unsalted
pistachios (about 1¼ cups)

1 oz. (30 g) Maltosec
(tapioca maltodextrin)

1 tablespoon plus
1 teaspoon (20 ml) water

OLIVE OIL AND VANILLA GANACHE

Scant ½ cup (110 ml) first cold
pressed extra-virgin olive oil

1 vanilla bean (preferably
Madagascar vanilla)

⅓ cup (2.6 oz. / 75 g)
whipping cream, 35% butterfat

3¾ oz. / 165 g white
couverture chocolate

PISTACHIO-SCENTED GANACHE

½ cup (4 oz. / 110 ml) mascarpone

1 scant cup (7¾ oz. / 220 ml)
whipping cream, 35% butterfat

1½ tablespoons (20 g) sugar

1 tablespoon plus 1 scant
tablespoon (15 g) confectioners' sugar

1 teaspoon (5 ml) vanilla syrup

1½ oz. (40 g) pistachio paste

DECORATION

3½ oz. (100 g) pine nuts (about 1 cup)

3 Golden Delicious apples (in pieces)

A few candied olives, halved lengthwise

Caramelized pistachios

Ground pistachios

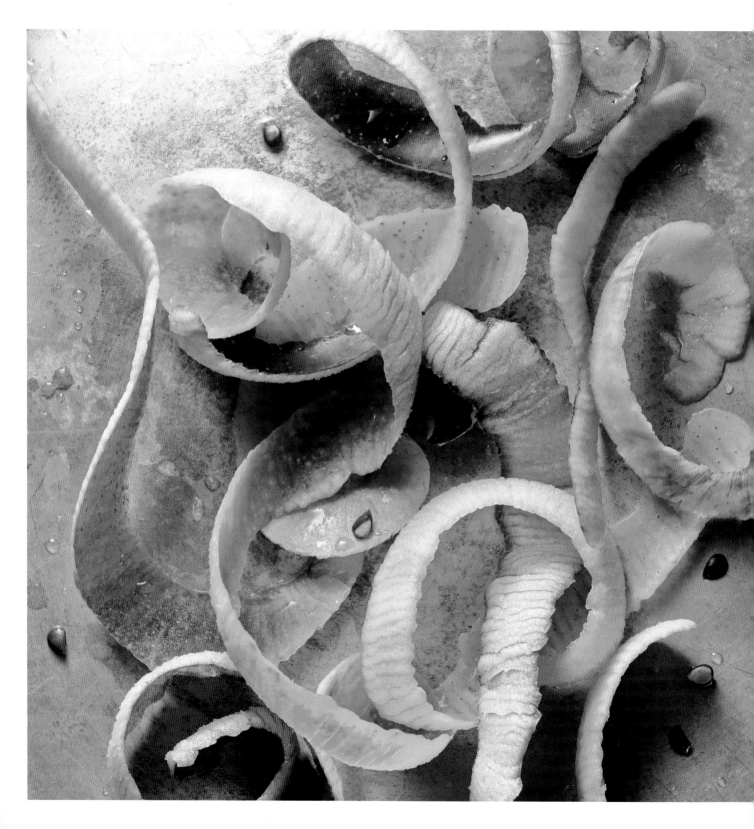

Apple Barlette

FOR THE SWEET HAZELNUT PASTE

Butter 10 éclair-shaped molds. Preheat the oven to 320°F (160°C) using the convection (fan-assisted) function.

In the bowl of a stand mixer fitted with the paddle attachment, combine the flour, salt, confectioners' sugar, ground vanilla, ground hazelnuts, potato starch, and butter. Combine until the mixture becomes grainy–a sandy texture (in French, this process is called *sablage*, sanding). Lastly, incorporate the egg.

Gather the paste into a ball and roll it out with a rolling pin.

Cut out oval shapes slightly larger than the molds. Line the molds with the paste and trim the edges. Bake for 15 to 20 minutes, until it is a lightly browned caramel color.

Reduce the heat to 270°F (130°C) for the caramelized pistachios.

FOR THE OLIVE OIL AND VANILLA GANACHE

Heat the olive oil to a temperature between 95°F and 104°F (40°C and 35°C); ensure it remains at this temperature.

Split the vanilla seed lengthwise and scrape out the seeds. Chop the couverture chocolate and melt it, either in the microwave oven or over a hot water bath.

In a saucepan over medium heat, bring the cream to a boil with the vanilla bean and seeds. Remove the bean and strain the mixture through a fine-mesh sieve into a bowl. Weigh this heated cream, and pour in a little more to reach the weight originally called for (some will have been lost in evaporation).

Pour this warm cream over the couverture chocolate, then stir in the warm oil. Stir to combine and place in the refrigerator.

FOR THE PISTACHIO-SCENTED GANACHE

In a container that you can fit with an airtight lid, combine all the ingredients using an immersion blender. Close the container and allow to rest in the refrigerator.

FOR THE CARAMELIZED PISTACHIOS

Combine the pistachios, Maltosec, and water to make a sticky paste. Spread it between two silicone baking sheets and bake for 25 minutes. (If you don't have two silicone baking sheets, you can use wax paper, but the paste will not caramelize as well.)

Increase the oven temperature to 350°F (175°C) for finishing.

TO FINISH AND ASSEMBLE

Spread the pine nuts over a baking sheet and roast at 350°F (175°C) for 8 minutes. Remove from the baking sheet and allow to cool.

Cut the apples into thin slices of the shape of your choice.

Soften the olive oil and vanilla ganache slightly in the microwave oven, but make sure that it remains chilled. Spread it over the baked sweet hazelnut paste base. Arrange the roasted pine nuts over the ganache, setting aside a few to decorate the tops.

With a whisk or electric beater, whip the pistachio-scented ganache. Spoon it into a pastry bag fitted with a plain 1/3-inch (8.5 mm, also known as U6) tip and pipe it over the length of each pastry.

Garnish with apple slices, candied olives, caramelized pistachios, and a few toasted pine nuts.

Dust with ground pistachios.

To garnish this pizza, choose a variety that is firm, with a delicate texture. Granny Smiths will give a good sweet-sour contrast, but you can go for Golden Delicious if you prefer more sweetness. In fact, you can use any other variety of apple you have at hand: this is an easy-going recipe.

Apple Pizza

MAKES ONE 12-INCH (30-CM) PIZZA

PIZZA DOUGH

1 scant cup (2½ oz. / 75 g)
cake flour (French T45)

½ cup minus 1 tablespoon (2 oz.
/ 50 g) all-purpose flour

0.1 oz. (3 g) fresh yeast

3 tablespoons (50 ml) water at 72°F (22°C)

¼ teaspoon (1 g) fine sea salt

½ teaspoon (2 g) sugar

1½ tablespoons extra virgin olive oil

1 tablespoon plus
1 teaspoon (20 ml) cold water

SALTED BUTTER CARAMEL

⅓ plus 1 tablespoon (90 ml) whipping cream, 35% butterfat

⅛ teaspoon (1 g) fleur de sel,
or other flaky sea salt

1 oz. (30 g) glucose syrup
(about 1½ tablespoons)

¾ cup (5 oz. / 150 g) sugar

2 tablespoons (25 g) unsalted
butter, in small cubes

ASSEMBLY

3 apples

Apple Pizza

FOR THE PIZZA DOUGH

Combine the two types of flour. Make a starter by combining the yeast with the warm water and 2½ tablespoons (25 g) of the flour mix. Allow to ferment for about 30 minutes in a warm place, until bubbles start to form at the surface.

Combine the remaining flour with the salt, sugar, and olive oil. Gradually stir in the fermented yeast, and then the cold water. Knead at length, until the dough is smooth and very soft, and no longer clings to your fingers. Shape it into a ball, place it in a mixing bowl four times bigger than it, and cover with plastic wrap or a clean, damp cloth. If you use a cloth, dampen it regularly while the dough rises.

The time the dough takes to rise depends on the room temperature. It should rise for at least 6 to 8 hours at 68°F (20°C), and up to 15 hours at 60°F (15°C). It should double in volume, and may even triple.

FOR THE SALTED BUTTER CARAMEL

Combine the cream with the fleur de sel and bring to a boil. Cook the glucose syrup and sugar together until they form a brown caramel. Deglaze with the warm cream and then stir in the butter.

TO ASSEMBLE AND COOK THE PIZZA

Preheat the oven to 480°F (250°C).

Roll the pizza dough into a 12-inch (30-cm) disk and place it on a baking sheet. Spread the salted butter caramel, stopping ¾ inch (2 cm) short of the rim. Wash and dry the apples and slice them thinly using a mandoline with safety guard. Arrange the apple slices over the pizza (see photo, page 55). Place in the oven, reduce the temperature to 350°F (180°C) and bake for 20 to 25 minutes, keeping an eye on the color. The apples should not darken too much.

Serve hot.

I f you use pre-rolled store-bought puff pastry, you will need at least three rolls to line ten Camembert boxes. When you are selecting the apples, bear in mind that red-skinned varieties are particularly attractive here. Go for Belle de Boskoop, Antarès®, Royal Gala, Juliet, Ariane, Melrose, Idared, Jonagored, or any others you may find. The only variety we advise against using are the American Reds, which are not suitable for pastry-making.

Apple Tartlets

IN CAMEMBERT BOXES

MAKES 10 TARTLETS

PUFF PASTRY
2¾ cups (12½ oz. / 350 g) all-purpose flour, plus more for dusting
1¼ teaspoons (7 g) fine sea salt
¾ cup (180 ml) cold water
2⅔ sticks (10 ½ oz. / 300 g) butter
or
1½ lb. (750 g) store-bought puff pastry, made with pure butter
Confectioners' sugar for dusting

APPLE FILLING
10 red apples
4½ sticks (1 lb. 2 oz. / 500 g) butter, melted
¾ cup (5 oz. / 150 g) sugar

SPECIAL EQUIPMENT
10 clean, empty Camembert boxes

FOR THE PUFF PASTRY

Sift the flour into the bowl of a stand mixer. Make a well in the center and fit on the dough hook. Dissolve the salt in the cold water and pour it into the well. Knead the ingredients together for 2 minutes at low speed, just until the dough no longer sticks to the side of the bowl. (At this stage, it is known as the détrempe, the water dough, and is the initial component of classic puff pastry.) Shape it into a ball and make a cross-shaped incision at the top to help the dough relax. Cover in plastic wrap to prevent a crust from forming on the surface and place in the refrigerator to chill for 1 to 2 hours.

Prepare the butter: using a rolling pin, pound the butter until it is malleable and shape it into a square (make sure the thickness is even). Place it in the refrigerator to firm up for about 1 hour so that it is the same texture as the water dough when the two are combined.

Lightly dust the work surface with flour and roll the water dough out using the rolling pin: spread out each of the four corners to make a tip and keep the central part of the dough thicker than the rest. This means you must roll the dough out at each of the four opposite corners. Place the square of butter in the center, with each corner at ½ inch (1 cm) from the edge.

Enclose the butter by folding each of the four corners of the water dough over it; the folded dough should not overlap and the butter must be entirely covered. It is now time to make the turns and folds (this is called the tourage).

Apple Tartlets

IN CAMEMBERT BOXES

FIRST TURN

When the butter is completely enclosed, even out the dough by rapping it lightly and regularly in both directions with the rolling pin (down the length and across the width). The dough should be a square, which makes it easy to roll out evenly into a rectangle. Now roll this into a rectangle, with a length three times the width; the thickness should be just under ½ inch (1 cm).

Brush off any excess flour. Fold the dough into three and use the rolling pin to lightly seal the three layers together. Rotate the dough a quarter-turn, placing the fold either on the right or on the left. Turn the fold inward, barely ¼ inch (5 mm) to make sure that it does not protrude when you make the second turn.

Cover the dough in plastic wrap and place it in the refrigerator to rest for at least 2 hours.

The procedure you have just undertaken is called a simple turn.

SECOND TURN

Seal each edge of the dough before you begin making the second turn so that the leaves of pastry inside do not move.

Following the instructions for the first turn, roll the dough out evenly. Fold the dough over into three. You have now made two turns. Cover in plastic wrap and place in the refrigerator to rest for at least 2 hours.

THIRD, FOURTH, AND FIFTH TURNS

Make two more turns, identical to those made previously. The dough has now undergone four turns. Cover in plastic wrap and place in the refrigerator to rest for at least 2 hours.

Make a last turn and chill again for 2 hours, until needed.

MAKE THE TARTLET CRUSTS

Preheat the oven to 350°F (180°C). Roll the dough to a thickness of no more than ⅛-inch (2.5 cm). Place it on a parchment-lined baking sheet and dust with confectioner's sugar over the entire surface. Cover the dough with another sheet of baking or parchment paper, and place another baking sheet over the top. This ensures that the puff pastry rises evenly. Bake for 30 minutes. Remove the puff pastry from the oven and reduce the temperature to 340°F (170°C) for the next step.

If you are using pre-rolled puff pastry, unroll them and place on a baking sheet (or two, if necessary) and place another baking sheet over it, as explained for the homemade puff pastry. You may need to bake the pastry in several batches.

Cut the puff pastry into ten 4-inch-diameter (10-cm) disks, or the size you need to fit your boxes.

FILL AND BAKE THE TARTLETS

Wash and dry the apples. Cut each apple into two, then, using a vegetable peeler or Japanese mandoline, cut them into fine slices. Cover the puff pastry disks with the slices, starting from the rim and making a spiral. The apple slices should rest on their straight edges. Brush the tops with one-quarter of the melted butter and sprinkle with half of the sugar.

Bake for 25 minutes.

Leaving the oven at the same temperature, take the tartlets out. Brush them once again with one-quarter of the melted butter and sprinkle with the remaining sugar.

Return them to the oven and bake for a further 25 minutes. Leaving the oven at the same temperature, brush the tartlets with the remaining butter and return to the oven for 15 minutes.

Serve warm or cold.

Sweet, firm, flavorful apples pair well with the buttery cookie crust. Opt for varieties such as the Chantecler, King of Pippins, Gala, Cox Orange Pippin, Jonagold, or Golden Delicious.

Breton Shortcrust Tart with Softened Apples

MAKES ONE 6½-INCH (16-CM) TART

BRETON SHORTCRUST PASTRY

½ cup plus 1 tablespoon (2½ oz. / 70 g) flour
1½ teaspoons (6 g) baking powder
1 egg yolk (20 g), the equivalent of
1 tablespoon plus 1 teaspoon
¼ cup (2 oz. / 50 g) sugar
3 tablespoons (50 g) salted butter, softened

PAN-FRIED APPLE CUBES

3 fairly large apples
3 tablespoons (50 g) salted butter
3 tablespoons light brown sugar

APPLE JELLY

⅓ cup (2½ oz. / 75 g) sugar
¾ teaspoon (1.5 g agar agar powder)
⅔ cup (150 ml) unsweetened hard apple cider
⅔ cup minus 2 teaspoons
(140 ml) artisanal apple juice

FOR THE BRETON SHORTCRUST PASTRY

Sift the flour with the baking powder. In a mixing bowl, whisk the egg yolk with the sugar until frothy. Whisk in the butter, then the dry ingredients. Cover in plastic wrap and allow to rest in the refrigerator while you prepare the apples.

FOR THE PAN-FRIED APPLE CUBES

Peel and core the apples. Cut two of the apples into 8 wedges and cut the third apple into small cubes. Set the cubes aside. Melt the butter in a skillet and add the sugar and then the apple pieces. Cook, stirring from time to time, until the apple pieces are lightly caramelized. Lightly pan fry the cubes

APPLE JELLY

(You can make this while the baked crust with the apple pieces is in the freezer.)

Combine the sugar and agar agar. Bring the hard cider and apple juice to a boil. Stir in the sugar and agar agar and bring to a rolling boil. Allow to boil for 3 minutes over high heat. Pour the mixture into a bowl and allow to cool to no less than 85°F (30°C).

TO ASSEMBLE AND BAKE

Preheat the oven to 340°F (170°C). Butter the tart ring and place it on a baking sheet lined with parchment paper. (Alternatively, use a pan with a removable bottom.)

Spread the Breton pastry evenly into the circle. Smooth it down well and arrange the apple eighths around in a rose shape. Bake for 25 minutes. Press down lightly on the surface of the tart so that the apples are slightly below the rim of the tart ring. Allow to cool, then arrange the apple cubes over the surface. Place in the freezer for at least 30 minutes. Remove the tart from the freezer and pour a little jelly between the crust and the rim of the ring. Place in the refrigerator for a few minutes until set. Pour the remaining jelly over the surface of the tart; it should reach the top of the rim. Chill for 1 hour and carefully remove the tart ring.

The small cubes of apple enhance these delicious cookies, adding a soft, refreshing note. The variety is entirely up to you: all apples that can be used for baking are suitable.

Apple Cookies

MAKES ABOUT 4½ LB. (2 KG) COOKIES

2 cups (8½ oz. / 240 g) self-rising flour
1 cup plus 1 scant cup (8½ oz. / 240 g) all-purpose flour
2 teaspoons baking powder
1 tablespoon baking soda
1 pinch salt
2 sticks plus 4 tablespoons (10 oz. / 285 g) salted butter, softened
Seeds of 1 vanilla bean
1½ cups (10 oz. / 285 g) light brown sugar
1½ cups (10 oz. / 285 g) sugar
3 eggs, at room temperature
3 apples
1 lb. 4 oz. (570 g) chocolate, 60% cacao

Sift the two types of flour, baking powder, baking soda, and salt together in a mixing bowl.

In a stand mixer fitted with the paddle attachment, or using an electric beater, cream the butter with the vanilla seeds and the two types of sugar. When thoroughly combined, add the eggs, one by one, and then the sifted dry ingredients. Stop when just combined.

Preheat the oven to 350°F (180°C). Line a baking sheet with parchment paper or a silicone baking mat.

Peel the apples and cut them into small dice. Chop the chocolate roughly to make large chips.

Drop spoonfuls of cookie dough (the best tool to use is an ice cream scoop for even sizes) 2 inches (5 cm) in diameter on the prepared baking sheet, leaving sufficient space for them to spread.

Arrange the apple cubes and chocolate pieces over the surface of all of the cookies, pressing them in lightly.

Bake for about 10 minutes, keeping an eye on how they color: they should be lightly golden, but not dark. Immediately transfer them to a cooling rack with a spatula. Allow to cool completely and store in an airtight container.

This fruity burger requires some preparation ahead of time: make the brioche dough and jelled raspberry the day before, as well as the thick caramel sauce. You will need two varieties of apple: any sort of Pippin, as long as it is a good size, for the caramelized apples, but the King of Pippins or large Chantecler would also be just perfect. The raw Granny Smith (which must also be large) adds a tangy note, freshness, and crunch. The components of a good burger should always be well balanced, after all.

Apple Burger

MAKES 8 BURGERS

BRIOCHE DOUGH
2 teaspoons (10 g) fine salt
3½ tablespoons (1½ oz. /
40 g) sugar
4 cups (13 oz. / 370 g) pastry
flour, plus more for dusting
1 cup (9 oz. / 250 g) egg, lightly beaten,
the equivalent of 5 large eggs
½ oz. (15 g) fresh yeast, crumbled
2⅔ sticks (10½ oz. / 300 g) butter, at
a room temperature, in small dice

JELLED RASPBERRY LAYER
7 oz. (200 g) fresh raspberries
1 cup minus 2½ tablespoons
(6 oz. / 170 g) sugar
0.28 oz. (5 g) pectin combined with 1½
tablespoons (20 g) sugar (see Note)
1 teaspoon (5 ml) lemon juice

THICK CARAMEL SAUCE
⅔ cup (4½ oz. / 125 g) sugar
1 tablespoon plus 1 teaspoon (20 ml) water
Scant ⅓ cup (70 ml) lemon juice
1 generous pinch salt

EGG WASH
⅓ cup (3½ oz. / 100 g) egg yolks, the
equivalent of 5 egg yolks, plus scant
½ cup (3½ oz. / 100 g) egg, lightly
beaten, the equivalent of 2 eggs
Scant ½ cup (2½ oz. / 75 g) white and
black sesame seeds for sprinkling

FILLING
4 large Pippin apples
5 tablespoons (2½ oz. / 75 g) salted butter
⅓ cup (2¼ oz. / 65 g) light brown sugar
3 balls burrata cheese
1 large Granny Smith apple

Note: Pectin may differ from one
country to another. Follow the directions
on your pectin packaging to firmly
set this quantity of raspberries.

Apple Burger

MAKE THE BRIOCHE DOUGH (A DAY AHEAD)

Place the salt and sugar in the bowl of a stand mixer fitted with the dough hook, then cover these ingredients with the flour.

Briefly beat the eggs with the yeast until it has completely dissolved. Set aside for 5 minutes.

Pour two-thirds of the egg-yeast mixture over the flour. Working at medium speed, knead it in until the dough gains elasticity. Continue until it pulls away from the sides of the bowl, then pour in the remaining egg-yeast mixture and knead until the dough again pulls away from the sides of the bowl.

Incorporate the butter and continue kneading until the dough is smooth and shiny. Lightly dust a large bowl with flour and transfer the dough into it. Immediately dust the surface with flour, and cover with plastic wrap directly in contact with the dough. Allow to rise at room temperature until doubled in volume, about 2 hours. In winter, leave the dough in a warm place.

Take the dough from the bowl and knock out the air bubbles that have accumulated by pressing it down from the center outward until it returns to its initial volume. Shape it into a ball, return it to the bowl, dust the surface with flour, cover with plastic wrap in direct contact with the top, and place in the refrigerator to rest until the next day.

If you are making the dough on the day that you will be baking it, chill it for a minimum of 2 hours before using it.

FOR THE JELLED RASPBERRY LAYER (A DAY AHEAD)

In a blender, process the raspberries with the sugar. Pour the mixture into a saucepan over medium heat and cook to 105°F (40°C). Add the pectin-sugar mixture and heat further, stirring continuously, until the mixture reaches 220°F (105°C). Remove from the heat and stir in the lemon juice. When thoroughly combined, pour over a silicone baking mat and allow to set overnight in the refrigerator.

FOR THE THICK CARAMEL SAUCE (A DAY AHEAD)

In a heavy-bottomed saucepan over medium heat, cook the sugar and water until the mixture forms a light brown caramel. Remove from the heat and stir in first the lemon juice, and then the salt. Whisk briefly and allow to cool. Transfer to a container, cover, and place in the refrigerator.

BAKE THE BRIOCHE BUNS

On the day of serving, make the egg wash: whisk the egg yolks with the eggs.

Divide the dough into eight equal parts. Shape each one into a ball and place on a baking sheet lined with parchment paper, spacing them out well. Brush with the egg wash (you will need more later) and allow to rise at room temperature for 45 minutes, until doubled in volume. Preheat the oven to 350°F (180°C).

Once again, brush the brioches with the egg wash and sprinkle with the sesame seeds. Bake for 15 to 20 minutes, until a lovely golden color. Remove from the baking sheet and allow to cool.

ASSEMBLE THE BURGERS

Peel the Pippin apples and core them. Cut them thinly into neat round slices. Melt the butter in a skillet over medium-high heat and add the apple slices. Cook for 3 minutes, then add the brown sugar. Stirring carefully so as not break the apple slices, allow them to caramelize. Remove from the heat.

Slice the burrata. Using a cookie cutter of the same diameter as the brioches, cut rounds of jelled raspberry.

Wash and dry the Granny Smith apple and cut it into thin rounds.

Cut each brioche into two. Spread a thin layer of caramel sauce over the bottom half and place a slice of jelled raspberry paste over that. Continue with a slice of burrata, a slice of Granny Smith, and a slice of caramelized Pippin.

To finish, spread a thin layer of caramel sauce over the top half of each brioche and close up the burgers.

Apple Tart

MAKES ONE 8½-INCH (22 CM) TART FOR 8

PAN-FRIED APPLES
2 Golden Delicious or Chantecler apples
3 tablespoons (2 oz. / 50 g) butter
2½ tablespoons (1 oz. / 30 g) light brown sugar

BRETON BUCKWHEAT PASTRY CRUST
½ cup (3½ oz. / 100 g) sugar
3 egg yolks
7 tablespoons (3½ oz. / 100 g) unsalted butter, softened
⅔ cup (3 oz./ 80 g) all-purpose flour
⅓ cup (2 oz. / 60 g) buckwheat flour
2 teaspoons (8 g) baking powder
⅛ teaspoon (1 g) fleur de sel, or other flaky sea salt
⅓ oz. (10 g) finely grated orange zest, about 1 tablespoon plus 2 teaspoons

APPLE CUBES
1 Granny Smith apple
Juice of 1 lemon

APPLE JELLY
1 cup (7 oz. / 200 g) sugar
0.11 oz. / 3 g agar agar powder
1¾ cups (420 ml) hard apple cider
1 cup plus scant ½ cup (340 ml) artisanal apple juice

This tart takes its inspiration from a Fauchon recipe. With interesting textural contrasts, its crusts include two typical Breton ingredients: buckwheat and fleur de sel. Use Golden Delicious or Chantecler apples for the softened layer on the Breton crust, and Granny Smith in small dice, raw, to set into the jelled layer. It's important to get the timing right for this recipe. Plan ahead: when the baked crust with the apple pieces has cooled, it must be placed in the freezer to chill for 30 minutes. During this time, you can dice the apple and make the apple jelly, which has to cool to a certain temperature (95°F / 35°C), at which point it must immediately be poured over the tart and allowed to set.

FOR THE PAN-FRIED APPLES
Peel the apples and core them with an apple corer. Cut into quarters and cut each quarter into halves. Melt the butter in a skillet over low heat. As soon as it is sizzling, arrange the apple pieces evenly in the skillet. Increase the heat to high and color the apple pieces on all sides. Sprinkle with the brown sugar and allow to caramelize lightly. Remove from the skillet and set aside.

FOR THE BRETON BUCKWHEAT PASTRY CRUST
Preheat the oven to 350°F (180°C).
In a mixing bowl, whisk the sugar with the egg yolks until pale, foamy, and thick. Gradually whisk in the butter. Sift the two types of flour with the baking powder. With a flexible spatula, fold the sifted ingredients into the yolk-sugar mixture, then incorporate the fleur de sel and orange zest. Butter an 8½-inch (22-cm) tart ring (or tart pan with removable bottom), 1 inch deep (2.5-cm) and place it on a baking sheet lined with baking or parchment paper. (This is not necessary if you are using a pan.) Using the cleaned flexible spatula, transfer the dough to the ring and smooth the surface. Arrange the apple pieces in a rose pattern over the dough. Bake for 35 to 45 minutes, keeping an eye on the color. The apples should not darken too much. Remove the baking sheet from the oven and allow the tart to cool in the ring, which you will need to leave in place to assemble the tart. Place the cooled tart in the freezer and allow to chill for 30 minutes.

FOR THE APPLE CUBES
Wash and dry the apple. Leaving the skin on, cut it into very small cubes (this is known as a *brunoise*). As you prepare the cubes, drizzle them with lemon juice to prevent them from browning.

FOR THE APPLE JELLY
Combine the sugar with the agar agar. Bring the hard cider and apple juice to a boil and stir in the sugar and agar agar. Allow to boil for 4 minutes. Remove from the heat and cool to 95°F (35°C), when it should be used immediately.

ASSEMBLE THE TART
On removing the tart from the freezer, scatter the apple cubes evenly over the top and immediately pour the jelly over, stopping just under ½ inch (1 cm) below the rim of the ring. Place in the refrigerator to chill and set for at least 30 minutes. Remove the ring and serve.

Apples and chestnuts are not often paired, but they make a fine duo, with chestnut honey adding a note that is rustic yet refined. All of the Pippin varieties, the Chantecler, and heirloom apples may be used for this recipe.

Roasted Apple in Chestnut Milk

SERVES 4

4 Pippin apples
2 eggs
Heaping ¼ cup (3½ oz. / 100 g) chestnut honey, or other richly flavored honey
1¼ cups (4½ oz. / 125 g) almond flour
5 tablespoons (3 oz. / 80 g) butter
10 fresh chestnuts
Scant ½ cup (100 ml) whole milk
Scant ½ cup (100 ml) whipping cream, 35% butterfat
7 oz. (200 g) chestnut spread (see Note)
Olive oil to taste

Note: Chestnut spread (*crème de marrons*) contains chestnuts, sugar, crushed candied chestnuts, glucose syrup, water (very little), and vanilla extract.

Preheat the oven to 350°F (180°C). Peel the apples and core them with a corer.

Whisk the eggs energetically with the honey to dissolve it completely. Dip the apples into the egg-honey mixture and then roll them in the almond flour to coat.

Place the apples in an ovenproof dish and dot with a few knobs of butter.

Bake for 30 to 40 minutes, depending on the size, until softened. You will need the oven at the same temperature to roast the chestnut chips.

FOR THE CHESTNUT CHIPS

While the apples are baking, remove the outer shells of the chestnuts with a small kitchen knife. Blanch them in boiling water for 2 to 3 minutes and drain.

When they are cool enough to handle, remove the skin with the knife tip. Cut the chestnuts into slices about ⅛-inch (3-mm) thick and place them on a baking sheet lined with parchment paper. Place in the oven for 15–20 minutes, until nicely browned, then remove.

FOR THE CHESTNUT MILK

Bring the milk and cream to a boil and pour over the chestnut spread. Whisk until combined.

Place each apple in the center of a large bowl. Pour the chestnut milk around, drizzle with a little olive oil, and garnish with the chestnut chips.

Here, a thermal shock is important when the tempura batter meets the hot oil (just as it is for the Apple Peel Tempura, page 46) so do have ice cubes at the ready to add to the batter. The best apples to use are firm ones with a good sweet-sour balance. We suggest Golden Delicious (the finest you can get), Chantecler, or any of the Pippins. For the accompanying fruit, you can use yellow kiwis, which are sweeter, tastier…and more expensive.

Plan ahead: make the tempura batter only when you are ready to begin frying.

Apple Tempura,

FORK-CRUSHED KIWI, AND VANILLA CREAM

SERVES 4

VANILLA CREAM
½ sheet (1 g) gelatin
1 vanilla bean
1 cup (250 ml) whole milk
Yolk of 1 extra large egg
¼ cup (2 oz. / 50 g) sugar
1½ tablespoons (½ oz. / 15 g) cornstarch
5 tablespoons (3 oz. / 80 g)
unsalted butter, softened

6 apples
4 kiwis

TEMPURA BATTER
1⅔ cups (7 oz. / 200 g) all-purpose flour
1 pinch salt
⅔ cup (3½ oz. / 100 g) potato starch
1⅔ cups (400 ml) hard apple cider, chilled
About 12 ice cubes

FOR FRYING
4 cups (1 liter) any neutral oil such as
grapeseed, sunflower, or Canola oil

Apple Tempura,

FORK-CRUSHED KIWI, AND VANILLA CREAM

FOR THE VANILLA CREAM

Soften the gelatin in a bowl of cold water for 10 minutes.

Split the vanilla bean lengthwise and scrape out the seeds with the tip of a knife.

In a heavy-bottomed saucepan, bring the milk to a boil. Add the vanilla bean and seeds. Remove from the heat, cover the saucepan, and allow to infuse for about 20 minutes.

In a mixing bowl, energetically whisk the egg yolk with the sugar until the mixture is pale and thick. Whisk in the cornstarch to combine thoroughly.

Remove the vanilla bean from the milk and pour some of the milk gradually over the yolk, sugar, and cornstarch mixture, whisking constantly. Return the mixture to the saucepan. Over medium-low heat, bring to a boil, whisking constantly. Remove from the heat. Drain the water from the gelatin sheet and stir it in until completely dissolved. Allow the cream to cool to 105°F (40°C). Stir in the butter, then process briefly with an immersion blender to create an emulsion. Transfer the vanilla cream to a bowl and cover with plastic wrap, pressing it down on the surface to prevent a skin from forming. Place in the refrigerator to chill.

FOR THE APPLES AND KIWIS

When the vanilla cream has chilled, peel the apples and core them. Cut them into sticks the size of large French fries.

Peel the kiwis and crush them with a fork.

FOR THE TEMPURA BATTER

Sift the flour, salt, and potato starch together into a mixing bowl. Make a well in the center and gradually pour in the hard cider, stirring constantly to prevent lumps from forming. When smooth, add the ice cubes. The batter should be very cold when you are ready to fry the apple sticks.

FOR FINISHING

Heat the oil to 400°F (200°C) in a large pot or fryer. Line a dish with sheets of paper towel to drain the apple sticks. You may need more than one layer.

When the oil has reached the correct temperature, use tongs to dip the apple pieces into the batter, coating them entirely. Working in batches, drop the coated apple pieces into the hot oil, taking care not to burn yourself with spluttering oil. When the coated apple pieces are lightly colored, place them on paper towels to drain.

Place portions of the apple tempura on plates and serve accompanied by vanilla cream and fork-crushed kiwi.

Soft

Apple Pie

PIE DOUGH
3 cups (13 oz. / 375 g) all-purpose flour, plus extra for dusting
2 sticks (8 oz. / 225 g) unsalted butter, well chilled and diced
½ teaspoon salt
Scant ½ cup to ⅔ cup (100 to 150 ml) ice water

APPLE FILLING
7 to 8 medium apples
Juice of ½ lemon
½ teaspoon salt
½ cup (3½ oz. / 100 g) granulated or light brown sugar
1 tablespoon flour (make sure it's level)
1 teaspoon cinnamon

ASSEMBLY
7 tablespoons (3½ oz. / 100 g) butter, in thin slices
Crème fraîche or vanilla ice cream, for serving

As American as apple pie" goes the saying, yet the apple pie can be traced back to medieval times in Europe, and is also an iconic British recipe. Apple pie pops up in English literature for the first time when Elizabethan dramatist Robert Greene has a shepherd declare to his beloved: "thy breath is like the steeme of apple pies."

The classic French apple dessert is an open apple tart baked in a shallow tart pan, or in a ring—we are not in the habit of covering our fruit, often painstakingly arranged in decorative patterns. Here is our take on this comforting, universally liked pie (called a tourte) with a dough that we do not brush with egg wash, to let its crumbly texture shine through.

Select apples that have a good sweet-sour balance: Belle de Boskoop, Chantecler, all the Pippins, and any of the heirloom varieties.

Apple Pie

FOR THE PIE DOUGH

If you are making the dough in a food processor, place the flour in the bowl and add the butter and salt. Process the ingredients together using short pulses, until the butter is incorporated into the flour and the texture is that of coarse cornmeal. Add the water, tablespoon by tablespoon, continuing to pulse. Stop when the dough comes together into a ball; it should be slightly soft but not wet. Lightly flour your hands and gather the dough into two balls, one slightly larger than the other. Flatten them both lightly, cover in plastic wrap, and place in the refrigerator to rest for 1 to 2 hours.

If you are using two knives to make the dough, combine the flour, butter, and salt in a large mixing bowl. Holding one knife in each hand, cross them like a pair of scissors and saw them back and forth. When all the butter has been incorporated into the flour and the mixture has a uniformly grainy texture, gradually add the water, continuing to cut through the ingredients with the knives, until they come together into a ball. Lightly flour your hands and follow the directions above to make two disks of dough.

It is important to handle the dough as little as possible with your hands.

FOR THE APPLE FILLING

Peel and core the apples. Cut each apple into quarters and each quarter into two pieces. Place them in a mixing bowl and stir in the lemon juice and salt. In a small bowl, combine the sugar, flour, and cinnamon. Stir into the apples to combine well.

ASSEMBLE AND BAKE THE PIE

Preheat the oven to 350°F (180°C).

Roll the two disks of dough to a thickness of about ⅛-inch (3 to 4 mm). Line the pie dish with the larger piece of dough, leaving some overhang around the rim. Spread the apples evenly over the base. Dot the slices of butter evenly over the surface of the apple layer.

Lightly dampen the edges of the dough and fit the other disk of rolled out dough over the pie dish. Pinch the dough together well, removing any excess (you will need a small amount to make the pie vent). If you wish, you can make a fluted pattern with a chopstick or the tines of a fork: this seals the two layers of dough together more firmly.

In the center of the top layer of dough, carefully pierce a small hole. Shape a piece of leftover dough into a tube and fit it over the hole, dampening it with a little water so that it fits in snugly. This vent enables the liquid from the apples to evaporate as the pie bakes.

Bake for 40 to 45 minutes, until a light golden color.

Serve hot with crème fraîche or vanilla ice cream.

Use this apple caviar to decorate your desserts, tapas, or any other dish of your choice.

Apple Caviar

MAKES ABOUT 1 LB. 2 OZ. (500 G)

4 cups (1 liter) grapeseed oil
⅓ cup (75 ml) water
⅓ cup (2½ oz. / 75 g) sugar
12 oz. (345 g) defrosted Granny Smith apple purée
or
the same weight in freshly juiced Granny Smith apples
0.46 oz. (13 g) agar agar powder, the equivalent of 6½ teaspoons, but best weighed accurately

SPECIAL EQUIPMENT
A pipette or syringe

Pour the grapeseed oil into a large mixing bowl and place it in the refrigerator.

In a large saucepan, bring the water and sugar to a boil and allow to cool completely.

Incorporate the purée or juice into the syrup and then whisk in the agar agar until smooth. Return to low heat and bring to a boil.

Have the bowl of chilled grapeseed oil at hand.

Draw the mixture into the pipette and push down the plunger, drop by drop, into the grapeseed oil. The drops will set instantly.

Drain them in a fine-mesh sieve, transfer to a container, and store in the refrigerator until needed.

For this multi-component recipe, begin by making the two creams: the Granny Smith cream and the Madagascar vanilla cream. They both require a two-hour chilling period. Then make the choux pastry, pipe out the éclairs, and bake them. Lastly, prepare the glaze and chocolate stems.

Vanilla and Granny Smith Éclairs

MAKES TEN 5-INCH (11-CM) ÉCLAIRS

GRANNY SMITH CREAM
Scant ½ teaspoon (2 g) powdered gelatin, 200 bloom
2 teaspoons (10 ml) cold water
3½ oz. (100 g) puréed Granny Smith apples
Generous ½ cup (4½ oz. / 130 g) lightly beaten egg
½ cup (3½ oz. / 100 g) sugar
1¾ sticks (6½ oz. / 190 g) butter
2 oz. (55 g) Sosa® green apple paste
1½ teaspoons (8 g) Manzanita® liqueur (a Granny Smith liqueur)

MADAGASCAR VANILLA CREAM
Scant cup (225 ml) milk
⅔ oz. (20 g) Madagascar vanilla bean, split lengthwise and seeds scraped
1 tablespoon plus 2 teaspoons (1 oz. / 30 g) egg yolk (about 1½ yolks)
¼ cup (2 oz. / 50 g) sugar
1½ tablespoons (½ oz. / 15 g) cornstarch or custard powder
5 tablespoons (3 oz. / 80 g) unsalted butter, diced

CHOUX PASTRY
⅔ cup (160 ml) whole milk
⅔ cup (160 ml) water
1 stick plus 3 tablespoons (5½ oz. / 160 g) unsalted butter
1½ teaspoons (6 g) sugar
¾ teaspoon (4 g) fine salt
1½ teaspoons (8 g) vanilla extract
1¼ cups (5½ oz. / 160 g) all-purpose flour
1¼ cups (10 oz. / 280 g) lightly beaten egg (about 5½ eggs)

VANILLA AND APPLE GLAZE
2 sheets (4 g) gelatin
¾ cup (200 ml) whipping cream, 35% butterfat
Scant ½ cup (3 oz. / 92 g) sugar
1 heaping tablespoon (1 oz. / 26 g) glucose syrup
2 tablespoons (33 ml) water
1 oz. (25 g) white chocolate, chopped
Green and yellow Maillard® coloring or other powdered food coloring of your choice
⅓ oz. (10 g) Sosa® green apple paste
A pinch of ground vanilla seed

CHOCOLATE STEMS
1 oz. (30 g) couverture chocolate, 55% cocoa mass, preferably Équatorial Dark (for the chocolate stems)

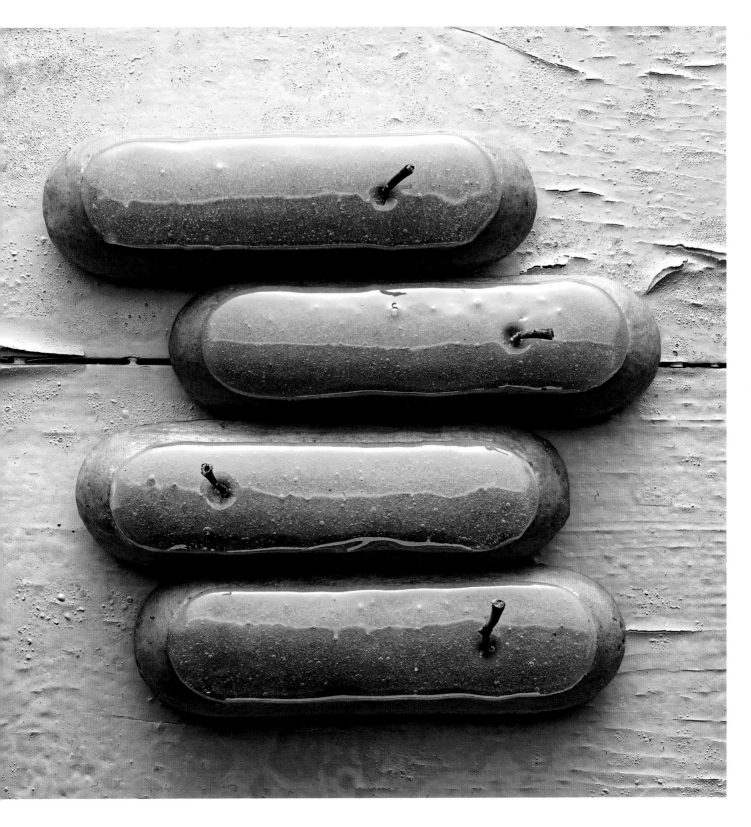

Vanilla and Granny Smith Éclairs

FOR THE GRANNY SMITH APPLE CREAM

Dissolve the gelatin in the cold water. Combine the Granny Smith apple purée, eggs, and sugar. Place over a hot water bath and cook, stirring frequently, until the temperature reaches 180°F (83°C).

Stir in the gelatin. When completely dissolved, allow the mixture to cool to 113°F (45°C). Add the butter, apple paste, and Manzanita®. Process with an immersion blender to combine. Transfer to a bowl, cover with plastic wrap pressed down on the surface, and place in the refrigerator for at least 2 hours before assembling the éclairs.

FOR THE MADAGASCAR VANILLA CREAM

Bring the milk to a boil with the vanilla bean and seeds. Remove from the heat, cover the saucepan with plastic wrap, and allow to infuse for 20 minutes. Strain through a fine-mesh sieve into a bowl. In a mixing bowl, whisk the egg yolk, sugar, and cornstarch. Whisk in the vanilla-infused milk. Return all the liquid to the saucepan over medium-low heat. Stirring constantly, bring to a boil. Allow the cream to cool to 105°F (40°C), then incorporate the butter. Process with an immersion blender and transfer to a bowl. Store in the refrigerator for at least 2 hours before assembling the éclairs.

FOR THE CHOUX PASTRY

In a large saucepan, bring the milk, water, butter, sugar, salt, and vanilla extract to a boil. As soon as it reaches a boil, pour in all of the flour at once, remove from the heat, and stir vigorously with a spatula, continuing until the batter pulls away from the sides of the saucepan. Preheat the oven to 480°F (250°C) using the convection (fan-assisted) setting or preheat a conventional oven to 350°F (175°C).(Instructions below).

Transfer the batter to the bowl of a stand mixer fitted with the paddle attachment, and add the eggs gradually, to form a smooth emulsion.

Spoon the batter into a pastry bag fitted with a 16 mm tip (between 12 and 16 teeth), and pipe 5-inch- (11-cm-) long éclairs on a parchment-lined baking sheet.

When the oven temperature is at exactly 480°F (250°C), switch it off, and place the éclairs in the oven. When the éclairs begin to swell and turn light brown, set the oven to 320°F (160°C) and bake for a further 15 minutes (approximately).

If you are using a conventional oven, bake the éclairs for about 30 minutes, without opening the door, until the éclairs are nicely puffed up and golden brown.

FOR THE VANILLA AND APPLE GLAZE

Soften the gelatin in a bowl of very cold water. Bring the cream to a simmer, then remove it from the heat. Heat the sugar, glucose syrup, and water to 320°F (160°C). Remove from the heat as soon as the mixture begins to color and deglaze immediately with the hot cream. Return to the heat and cook to between 215°F and 221°F (102°C and 105°C), the small thread stage. Stir in the white chocolate and allow to cool to lukewarm. At 160°F (70°C), drain the water from the gelatin and stir in until completely dissolved. Incorporate the coloring to achieve your desired shade. Process briefly with an immersion blender. Add the apple paste and the ground vanilla and process once again. Place in the refrigerator to chill.

FOR THE CHOCOLATE STEMS

Temper the chocolate and transfer it into a paper cone. Cut the tip and pipe small apple stems on a sheet of food-safe acetate; allow to set.

TO ASSEMBLE AND FINISH

Combine two-thirds of the Granny Smith apple cream with one-third of the vanilla cream. To fill, pierce three holes in the base and pipe in. Warm the glaze just enough for it to be fluid and dip the tops of the éclairs in it. Place a chocolate stem atop each éclair.

Apple Upside-Down Éclairs

ÉCLAIR TATIN

MAKES TEN 5-INCH (11-CM) ÉCLAIRS

MADAGASCAR VANILLA CREAM
Scant ¼ teaspoon (1 g) gelatin, 200 bloom
1 teaspoon cold water
Scant cup (225 ml) milk
⅔ oz. (20 g) Madagascar vanilla bean,
split lengthwise and seeds scraped
1 tablespoon plus 2 teaspoons (1 oz.
/ 30 g) egg yolk (about 1½ yolks)
¼ cup (2 oz. / 50 g) sugar
1½ tablespoons (½ oz. / 15 g)
cornstarch or custard powder
5 tablespoons (3 oz. / 80 g)
unsalted butter, diced

CHOUX PASTRY
⅔ cup (160 ml) whole milk
⅔ cup (160 ml) water
1 stick plus 3 tablespoons
(5½ oz. / 160 g) unsalted butter
1½ teaspoons (6 g) sugar
¾ teaspoon (4 g) fine salt
1½ teaspoons (8 g) vanilla extract
1¼ cups (5½ oz. / 160 g) all-purpose flour
1¼ cups (10 oz. / 280 g) lightly
beaten egg (about 5½ eggs)

TATIN-STYLE APPLES
4 Golden Delicious apples (you will
need 1 lb. / 400 g net when cubed)
Zest of ¼ orange
½ cup (3½ oz. / 100 g) sugar

CARAMEL GLAZE
¼ cup (2 oz. / 50 g) sugar
Scant ¼ cup (50 ml) very hot water
3 oz. (90 g) neutral glaze
(such as Marguerite®)

HAZELNUT STREUSEL
2½ tablespoons (1 oz. /
25 g) all-purpose flour
⅛ teaspoon (1 g) fleur de sel,
or other flaky sea salt
2 tablespoons (1 oz. / 25 g) sugar
¼ cup (2 oz. / 25 g) ground hazelnuts
1 tablespoon plus 2 teaspoons
(2 oz. / 25 g) butter, softened

FINISH
Edible gold leaf for decoration

90
SOFT

Apple Upside-Down Éclairs

ÉCLAIR TATIN

FOR THE MADAGASCAR VANILLA CREAM

Dissolve the gelatin in the water.

Bring the milk to a boil with the vanilla bean and seeds. Remove from the heat, cover the saucepan, and allow to infuse for 20 minutes. Strain through a fine-mesh sieve into a bowl. In a mixing bowl, whisk the egg yolk, sugar, and cornstarch. Whisk in the vanilla-infused milk. Return all the liquid to the saucepan over medium-low heat. Stirring constantly, bring to a boil. Allow the cream to cool to 105°F (40°C), then incorporate the butter. Process with an immersion blender and transfer to a bowl. Store in the refrigerator for at least 2 hours before assembling the éclairs.

FOR THE CHOUX PASTRY

In a large saucepan, bring the milk, water, butter, sugar, salt, and vanilla extract to a boil. As soon as it reaches a boil, pour in all of the flour at once, remove from the heat, and stir vigorously with a spatula, continuing until the batter pulls away from the sides of the saucepan. Preheat the oven to 480°F (250°C) using the convection (fan-assisted) setting or heat a conventional oven to 350°F (175°C).(Instructions below).

Transfer the batter to the bowl of a stand mixer fitted with the paddle attachment, and add the eggs gradually, to form an emulsion that is smooth.

Spoon the batter into a pastry bag fitted with a fill tip (between 12 and 16 teeth), and pipe 5-inch- (11-cm-) long éclairs on a baking sheet lined with parchment paper.

When the oven temperature is at exactly 480°F (250°C), switch it off, and place the éclairs in the oven. When the éclairs begin to swell and turn light brown, set the oven to 320°F (160°C) and bake for a further 15 minutes approximately.

If you are using a conventional oven, bake the éclairs for about 30 minutes, without opening the door. The éclairs should be golden brown.

FOR THE TATIN-STYLE APPLES

Preheat the oven to 350°F (180°C).

Wash and peel the apples. Cut them into ¾-inch (2-cm) dice. Grate the orange zest over the apple dice. Cook the sugar until it forms a well-colored caramel. Add the apples and stir well. Place in an ovenproof dish, cover, and bake for 30 minutes, stirring carefully halfway through. You will need the oven to be at the same temperature to bake the streusel.

FOR THE CARAMEL GLAZE

Begin by making a caramel syrup: Using the dry caramel method (see p. 186), cook the sugar until it is a well-colored caramel. Deglaze very carefully with the hot water (it might spatter) and allow to cool. When the syrup is cold, weigh ⅔ oz. (20 g) of it and whisk or stir it into the neutral glaze.

FOR THE HAZELNUT STREUSEL

Working with your fingertips, rub the flower, fleur de sel, sugar, hazlenuts, and butter together until they reach a uniformly grainy texture. Gather up the mixture into a ball and roll it to a thickness of ⅓-inch (7 mm). Transfer the streusel dough to a baking sheet and place in the refrigerator until very firm. Cut into cubes and bake on a baking sheet lined with parchment paper at 350°F (175°C) for 10 to 15 minutes, until golden and very crisp.

TO ASSEMBLE AND FINISH

Cut the éclairs horizontally, removing the top part. Scoop out the crumb of the éclair and, using a pastry bag, fill the bottom with the Madagascar vanilla cream. Arrange the Tatin-style apple cubes over the cream and brush them with the caramel glaze. Decorate with a few streusel crumbs and a little edible gold leaf.

A tart-tasting apple is ideal for this recipe: Belle de Boskoop, Reinette Grise du Canada, Granny Smith, or any tangy heirloom varieties you might be lucky to find—or just go ahead and use your favorite.

Apple-Calvados Cake

MAKES ONE 7- TO 7½-INCH
(18- TO 20-CM) CAKE FOR 6
(USE A SPRINGFORM PAN)

APPLES

2 large apples
1 tablespoon lemon juice
2 tablespoons (1 oz. / 30 g) butter
3 tablespoons Calvados or other apple brandy

BATTER

3 oz. (80 g) almond paste, 52% almonds
1 cup plus 2 tablespoons
(5 oz. / 150 g) all-purpose flour
Scant ½ cup (3 oz. / 80 g) sugar
1 scant tablespoon (11 g) baking powder
(if you are using French sachets, 1 sachet)
2 extra-large eggs (4 oz. / 120 g)
⅔ cup (150 ml) milk
5 tablespoons (3 oz. / 80 g)
unsalted butter, melted and cooled, plus
1 tablespoon (20 g) butter for the pan

TOPPING

5 tablespoons (3 oz. / 80 g) lightly
salted butter, well softened
4 tablespoons light brown sugar
½ teaspoon cinnamon

Apple-Calvados Cake

FOR THE APPLES

Peel the apples and cut them into thick slices, then into small dice. Drizzle them with the lemon juice, tossing them well, so that they do not brown.

Melt the butter in a skillet and sauté the apple cubes for 6 minutes, until golden, stirring carefully from time to time. Pour in the Calvados and carefully flambé the contents of the skillet.

FOR THE BATTER

Cut the almond paste into small cubes. Sift the flour.

In the bowl of a stand mixer fitted with the paddle attachment, place the sifted flour, sugar, and baking powder and beat just to combine. Add the eggs, one by one, then 1 tablespoon (20 ml) of the milk.

When smooth, swap the paddle attachment for the whisk and pour in the remaining milk. Scrape down the sides of the bowl with a scraper or flexible spatula to ensure that the milk is evenly incorporated. Whisk in the melted butter and stop when just combined.

Preheat the oven to 400°F (200°C).

Butter the base and sides of the springform pan. Cut out a disk of parchment paper the same diameter, butter it, and place it, butter side up, at the base of the pan. Pour the batter into the pan, then arrange the apple cubes evenly over it, without pushing them down.

Bake for 35 minutes, keeping an eye on the color.

FOR THE TOPPING

When the cake is almost baked, combine the salted butter with the light brown sugar and cinnamon. As soon as the cake is done, spread this mixture over the top.

This cake is a hybrid of the apple cake and apple upside-down cake, with the delightful addition of maple syrup. Use apples that are fairly firm—but not too firm—and with more tang than sweetness. Go for any of the Pippins, the Reinette Grise du Canada (Pomme Gris or Pomme Grise) in particular, if you can get hold of it, or the Belle de Boskoop, Braeburn, Melrose, or any heirloom variety.

Apple–Maple Syrup Cake

MAKES ONE 8- TO 9-INCH (10- TO 23-CM) CAKE FOR 8 TO 10

SYRUP
7 tablespoons (3½ oz. / 100 g) lightly salted butter
1 tablespoon plus 2 teaspoons (25 ml) maple syrup

CAKE
1½ cups (6⅓ oz. / 180 g) all-purpose flour
1¼ teaspoons (5.5 g) baking powder (if you are using French sachets, ½ sachet)
1½ sticks (6 oz. / 180 g) salted butter, softened, plus extra for the cake pan
1 cup plus 2 tablespoons (6 oz. / 180 g) maple sugar (or light brown sugar)
1 egg
¾ cup (200 ml) whole milk
Seeds of 1 vanilla bean
1 lb. 2 oz. (500 g) fairly small apples

Preheat the oven to 350°F (180°C). Butter a round cake pan.

FOR THE SYRUP

In a saucepan over low heat, gently melt the butter with the maple syrup. Bring to a simmer, and simmer very gently for 7 to 8 minutes. Remove from the heat.

FOR THE CAKE

Sift the flour with the baking powder. Place the butter and maple sugar in the bowl of a stand mixer fitted with the whisk and beat until the mixture is light and airy.

Add the egg and whisk for a few more minutes.

Add the milk and sifted flour and baking powder alternately, in several additions, whisking continuously. Whisk in the vanilla seeds.

Pour the syrup into the base of the cake pan.

Peel the apples and core them with an apple corer. Cut them into rounds and arrange the apples over the syrup to form an attractive pattern.

Pour in the batter and bake for 50 minutes. To test for doneness: the tip of a knife inserted into the center should come out dry. Remove from the oven and leave in the pan for 15 minutes before carefully turning it out. Serve at room temperature.

To counterbalance the sourness of the rhubarb, select a sweet variety of apple such as Golden Delicious, Gala, Chantecler, or Jonagold.

Apple, Rhubarb, and Polenta Cake

MAKES ONE 8-INCH (20-CM) CAKE FOR 6 TO 8

10 oz. (300 g) rhubarb
1 tablespoon sugar to cook with the rhubarb
2 medium apples
1½ cups (5 oz. / 150 g) almond flour
¾ cup (5 oz. / 150 g) sugar or pale cane sugar
½ cup minus 1 tablespoon (2 oz. / 50 g) all-purpose flour
1 teaspoon baking powder
3½ oz. (100 g) instant polenta (about a scant ½ cup)
⅔ cup (150 ml) Greek-style yogurt
4 eggs, lightly beaten
Finely grated zest and juice of 1 orange

Preheat the oven to 350°F (180°C). Line a square cake pan with parchment or baking paper.

Wash and dry the rhubarb; do not peel it. Cut it into 1½-inch (4-cm) chunks. In an ovenproof dish (preferably porcelain) combine the rhubarb pieces with the tablespoon of sugar and bake until tender, about 30 minutes.

Peel the apples and dice them. Combine the dice with the cooked rhubarb, stirring gently.

In a large mixing bowl, combine the almond flour, sugar, flour, baking powder, and polenta. Fold in the yogurt, eggs, and orange zest and juice.

Spread half of the apple-rhubarb mixture over the base of the pan. Pour in the batter, then carefully spread the remaining apple-rhubarb mixture over that. Bake for 45 minutes, until a cake tester inserted into the center comes out dry.

Turn the cake onto a rack and allow to cool before serving.

Thanks to the traditional earthenware cooking pot with its distinctive conical lid, the tagine, the apples are braised to tender, caramelized goldenness. Select firm apples such as Chantecler, Belle de Boskoop, Granny Smith, Rubinette, or Braeburn, but avoid Golden Delicious, which is too sweet and not sufficiently flavorful here. Your tagine dish should be a genuine one, not a dish that is simply varnished and decorated, meant for serving only. If you don't have one, use a sauté pan with a lid or a cast-iron pot.

Apple Tagine

SERVES 4

3 fairly large apples
Juice of ½ lemon
3 tablespoons (2 oz. / 50 g) unsalted butter
2 tablespoons light brown sugar
4 to 5 pods green cardamom, lightly crushed with the blade of a large knife
A few shards star anise
2 cinnamon sticks
2 dried figs, halved
4 dried apricots
2 tablespoons runny honey
1 tablespoon argan oil
4 fresh figs
3½ oz. (100 g) whole blanched almonds (about ¾ cup), lightly roasted

Peel and core the apples and cut them each into eight pieces. Rub them with the lemon juice.

Heat the tagine over medium heat. Melt the butter in the tagine, then pour in the brown sugar and add the apple pieces, crushed cardamom, star anise shards, and cinnamon sticks. Sauté the ingredients, stirring carefully with a wooden spoon, until the apples caramelize slightly, about 5 minutes. Add the dried figs and apricots.

Cover with the lid and cook for 20 minutes, without lifting up the lid. Combine the honey and argan oil with a few drops of water so that the mixture is fluid enough to pour.

Cut the fresh figs into quarters.

When the apple pieces are tender, remove the tagine from the heat and lift off the lid. Drizzle the honey–argan oil mixture over and stir it in carefully.

Add the fresh fig quarters and scatter with the roasted almonds.

Serve still warm or at room temperature.

To make this traditional Dutch tart with a custard base, select a variety of cooking apples, such as Belle de Boskoop, any of the Pippins, and in particular the Reinette Grise du Canada (Pomme Gris or Pomme Grise), Jonagold, or heirloom varieties.

Apple Custard Tart

MAKES ONE 8-INCH (20-CM) TART FOR 6 TO 8

TART DOUGH

2 cups (9 oz. / 250 g) all-purpose flour
⅔ cup (4½ oz. / 125 g) light brown sugar
1 pinch salt
Finely grated zest of 1 lemon
1 stick plus 2 tablespoons (5 oz. / 150 g) butter, chilled and diced, plus a little for the pan
Ice water

FILLING

1 lb. 2 oz. (500 g) apples
⅓ cup (2 oz. 50 g) sultanas (golden raisins)
2 eggs, plus 1 egg yolk for the egg wash
Scant ½ cup (100 ml) whole milk
3½ tablespoons (1½ oz. / 40 g) sugar
A little ground cinnamon
3 tablespoons cornstarch or custard powder
A little clear apricot jam (optional)

Combine the flour, brown sugar, salt, and lemon zest in a large mixing bowl. Using two knives, work in the butter, making sawing motions with the knives, until the mixture is a uniformly grainy texture. (Alternatively, use a pastry cutter.) Add just enough ice water for the dough to come together and carefully shape it into a ball. Do not handle it more than strictly necessary–it must remain soft.

Butter the tart pan and dust the work surface lightly with flour. Roll the dough into a disk about ¼ inch (7 mm) thick, setting aside a little to make small rolls of dough to top the tart with.

Line the tart pan with the dough, stopping just under ½ inch (1 cm) from the top of the rim.

Preheat the oven to 350°F (180°F),

Peel the apples, cut them into quarters, and remove the cores. Cut the quarters into slices or into cubes. Stir in the sultanas and spread the mixture out over the base of the tart.

Beat the whole eggs with the milk, sugar, cinnamon, and cornstarch. Pour the liquid over the fruit, ensuring that there are no gaps between the fruit pieces.

Roll the remaining dough into small balls or logs and dot them over the top of the tart.

Brush them with egg wash and bake for 50 minutes.

Allow to cool for 10 minutes. If you wish, brush the top with a little slightly heated smooth apricot jam.

Apples in Pastry Cases, Normandy Style

BOURDELOTS NORMANDS

SERVES 6

UNSWEETENED SHORT PASTRY CASE

1 cup plus 2 tablespoons (5 oz. / 150 g) all-purpose flour
1 stick plus 2 tablespoons (5 oz. / 150 g) butter, if possible raw butter, unsalted or lightly salted (if you use salted butter, omit the salt), chilled and diced
2 teaspoons (10 g) fine salt
Ice water

6 apples
1 tablespoon lemon juice
1 stick plus 2 tablespoons (5 oz. / 150 g) butter, if possible raw butter, softened
3 tablespoons light brown sugar
1 sachet vanilla sugar (see Note), or 1 teaspoon vanilla extract
1 generous pinch fine salt
Whipped cream or vanilla ice cream, for serving

Note: If you do not have vanilla sugar in sachets, keep in mind that it's simple to always have a jar in stock. Simply wash and dry a used vanilla bean and place it in a jar of sugar for at least one week. For one sachet use approximately 1 tablespoon of homemade vanilla sugar.

In Normandy, these specialties are made with Reinette Grise du Canada (Pomme Gris or Pomme Grise). Whatever you use, be sure to choose nice round apples, small- to medium-sized, that are firm and tart. The best are the heirloom varieties: all the Pippins, particularly the Bailleul, Clochard, and Patte-de-Loup. Sometimes, the butter stuffing is replaced with red currant or apple jelly (recipe, page 140). You can make this recipe using pears; the pastry then changes its name to *douillon*.

Apples in Pastry Cases, Normandy Style

BOURDELOTS NORMANDS

FOR THE PASTRY CASES

Place the flour, butter, and salt in the bowl of a food processor. Process the ingredients together using short pulses, until the butter is incorporated into the flour and the texture is that of coarse cornmeal. Continuing to pulse, add ice water tablespoon by tablespoon, until the dough comes together. Gather it into a ball, handling it as little as possible. Cover it in plastic wrap and place in the refrigerator to rest for 2 hours.

TO ASSEMBLE AND BAKE

Preheat the oven to 350°F (180°C).

Peel the apples, leaving them whole, and core them with an apple corer to make a cylindrical hole. Rub the apples with lemon juice so that they do not brown.

In a mixing bowl, combine the butter, brown sugar, vanilla sugar, and salt until they form a smooth paste.

Roll the dough out to a thickness of ⅛-inch (3 mm). Cut it into six squares large enough to encase the apples completely. Leave a small amount of dough to make 6 vents for the cases, and decorations if you wish.

Place each apple in the center of a dough square. With a teaspoon, fill the hollow with the butter-sugar paste. Wrap each apple with the dough, taking care not to crush it at all. Do not leave any openings! A few drops of water will be helpful in sealing the dough.

Make a very small hole at the top and surround it with a little dough so that moisture can escape during baking.

The pastry case is not brushed with egg wash, but generally decorated with dough cut into leaf shapes, which you can affix to it.

Place the wrapped apples on a baking sheet and bake for about 45 minutes, until the pastry is lightly colored–it should not darken too much.

Serve the apples in pastry cases still hot, but not too hot, with whipped cream or vanilla ice cream.

Pippins are perfect for these mini tartes Tatin. Try the King of Pippins, Reinette Clochard, and any regional Pippins you may find. The Chantecler also makes a good tartlet. The photo on the facing page shows three different ways of arranging the apples: in wedges, as explained in the recipe below; in small dice; and in fine slices. Use them as inspiration for your own creations. Plan your time carefully to include two hours of chilling for the apple domes and the brief rest for the puff pastry.

Individual Apple Upside-Down Tartlets

MAKES 6 TARTLETS

CARAMEL
1 cup plus 2½ tablespoons (8 oz. / 230 g) sugar

APPLE TOPPING
6 apples
½ cup (3½ oz. / 100 g) sugar
1 oz. (25 g) pectin NH

PASTRY BASE
7 oz. (200 g) Puff Pastry (see page 58)
or store-bought puff pastry sheets

SPECIAL EQUIPMENT
Six silicone hemispherical 3-inch (8-cm) molds

FOR THE CARAMEL

Using the dry method (see p. 186), make a medium-brown caramel with the sugar. Immediately pour it into the silicone molds.

FOR THE APPLE TOPPING

Preheat the oven to 320°F (160°C).

Peel and core the apples using a corer. Cut each one in half, and each half into 3 wedges.

Combine the sugar with the pectin NH and coat the apple pieces with the mixture. Fit them snugly into the cavities of the molds and cover with aluminum foil.

Bake for 40 minutes. (If you plan on baking the puff pastry soon after the apples, adjust the oven temperature to 350°F (180°C).

While the apple pieces are baking, roll out the puff pastry dough and prick the entire surface with a fork. Place in the refrigerator to chill for 20 minutes. Using a cookie cutter, cut out 3-inch (8-cm) disks.

Remove the baked apples from the oven. Leaving them in the molds, allow them to cool and place in the refrigerator for at least 2 hours.

Line a baking sheet with parchment paper and place the disks of puff pastry on it. Bake them at 350°F (180°C) for 30 minutes, or until golden and crisp, following the advice on page 61 to keep them flat. When they are cool, carefully turn the domes of apple out of their molds using a palette knife, and place them over the puff pastry disks.

Apple Clafoutis

WITH PECAN PRALINE AND CARAMELIZED PECANS

SERVES 6

PECAN PRALINE PASTE
6 oz. (180 g) shelled pecans, about 1¼ cu Pasteps
Scant ⅔ cup (4 oz. / 120 g) sugar
3 tablespoons (40 ml) water
½ teaspoon fleur de sel or other flaky salt

CLAFOUTIS BATTER
4 eggs
6 oz. (180 g) pecan praline paste
3 tablespoons (1¾ oz. / 50 g) butter, melted and cooled
¾ cup plus 2 tablespoons (3½ oz. / 100 g) all-purpose flour, sifted
1 pinch salt
1⅔ cups (400 ml) whole milk

6 apples

CARAMELIZED PECANS
5 oz. (150 g) shelled pecans, about 1 cup
Generous ½ cup (2¾ oz. / 75 g) confectioners' sugar

According to French purists, this recipe should not be considered a clafoutis, as it is not made with cherries, but rather as a *flognarde*, a specialty with apples from the same region, Limousin. But since apples are the subject of this book, we will continue to call it a clafoutis. Pippins, or any other tart apples, such as Belle de Boskoop or the Reinette Grise du Canada, will serve as a foil for the sweetness of both the clafoutis batter and the sweet crunchy pecans.

FOR THE PECAN PRALINE PASTE

Preheat the oven to 320°F (160°C). Spread the pecans over a baking sheet and roast them for about 15 minutes. They should be warm when you incorporate them into the caramel, so plan your timing carefully. In a large saucepan over medium heat, combine the sugar and water and cook until a brown caramel forms. Add the still-warm pecans to the caramel and stir in briskly. Then stir in the fleur de sel. When the pecans are completely coated, carefully spread them out on a silicone baking mat (the mixture will be very hot). Allow to cool completely, then break into small chunks. Process them in a food processor until ground to powder. Turn the mixer up to high speed and continue grinding until the mixture becomes a paste.

FOR THE CLAFOUTIS BATTER

In a mixing bowl, whisk the eggs. Whisk in the praline paste and then the melted butter. When incorporated, whisk in the flour and salt, and lastly, the milk.

BAKE THE CLAFOUTIS

Preheat the oven to 340°F (170°C). Peel and core the apples and cut them into a ¾-inch (2-cm) dice. Spread the dice over an ovenproof dish, preferably ceramic or porcelain. (You can also use a pie dish.) Pour the clafoutis batter over the apples and bake for 40 minutes, until it is fairly firm.

FOR THE CARAMELIZED PECANS

While the clafoutis is baking, chop the pecans roughly with a knife. Place them in a saucepan with the confectioners' sugar and set over medium heat. Stir constantly until the sugar caramelizes and coats the pecan pieces. Carefully transfer to a baking sheet to cool and then separate them into chunks.

TO FINISH

Allow the clafoutis to cool to lukewarm. Scatter the top with caramelized pecans.

Iceberg Meringues

SERVES 4

MERINGUE

5 egg whites, at room temperature
1 pinch salt
1¼ cups (9 oz. / 250 g) sugar
½ tonka bean, grated
¾ cup (3½ oz. / 100 g) confectioners' sugar

TO ASSEMBLE

9 oz. (250 g) Applesauce (see page 29)
7 oz. (200 g) white chocolate
1 cup minus 3 tablespoons (6¾ oz. / 190 g) mascarpone
¼ cup (60 ml) whipping cream, 35% butterfat

FOR THE MERINGUE

Preheat the oven to 230°F (110°C). Line a baking sheet with parchment paper.

In the bowl of a stand mixer at medium speed, whisk the egg whites with the pinch of salt, about one-third of the sugar, and the grated tonka bean. (You can also use an electric beater.)

When the whites begin to form peaks, add the remaining sugar and whisk at high speed until the mixture is firm and glossy.

Spread the meringue over the prepared baking sheet, sprinkle with the confectioners' sugar, and bake for 1 hour. Let cool.

TO FINISH AND ASSEMBLE

While the meringue is baking, you can prepare the applesauce if you don't already have it at hand. Allow it to cool.

Melt the white chocolate in the microwave oven or over a hot water bath. Turn the sheet of meringue over so that the side unsweetened with confectioners' sugar is facing upward. Spread a thin layer of melted chocolate over it–this provides a waterproof coating. Allow the chocolate to set.

Whisk the whipping cream into the mascarpone.

Using a serrated knife, cut the sheet of meringue into two equally sized pieces.

Spread one-half with the cool applesauce and the other half with the mascarpone-cream mixture. Sandwich the two halves together. Using the same knife, cut pieces to form iceberg-shaped meringue desserts.

Make the candied kumquats a day ahead. The recipe calls for only ten of these small citrus fruits, but it's worth making more to store in the refrigerator and use for other occasions–they are truly delicious. However, for the quantity of syrup given below, do not use more than 10 oz. (300 g) of fresh kumquats. As for the apples, you can use Rubinette, Antarès®, Juliet, Braeburn, all the Pippins, fine-quality Golden Delicious, or Chantecler.

Apple-Citrus Salad with Candied Kumquats

SERVES 4

CANDIED KUMQUATS
10 fresh kumquats
2 cups (14 oz. / 400 g) sugar
1¼ cups (300 ml) water

APPLE-CITRUS SALAD
3 apples
3 tablespoons (1¾ oz. / 50 g) lightly salted butter
Scant ⅓ cup (2 oz. / 60 g) light brown sugar
¾ cup (200 ml) artisanal apple juice
1 grapefruit
2 oranges

FOR THE CANDIED KUMQUATS

A day ahead, blanch the kumquats twice in boiling water to reduce their bitterness.

Make a syrup: Place the sugar and water in a saucepan and bring to a boil. Reduce the heat, add the kumquats to the syrup, cover with a disk of wax or parchment paper cut to the size of the saucepan, and simmer for 45 minutes.

Allow the kumquats to cool in the syrup and place in the refrigerator for at least 12 hours.

FOR THE APPLE-CITRUS SALAD

Peel and core the apples. Cut them into 8 wedges. Melt the butter in a skillet and sauté the apple wedges over high heat for 3 to 5 minutes, until nicely golden. Remove them from the skillet.

In the same skillet, heat the light brown sugar until it forms a brown caramel. Remove from the heat and immediately deglaze it with the apple juice (be careful not to burn yourself). Return the apples to the skillet with the caramel and place over medium heat. Reduce the liquid to a syrupy consistency, stirring from time to time–take care not to break up the apple pieces, which should remain whole.

While the contents of the skillet are on the heat, peel the grapefruit and oranges, leaving no traces of white pith. Cut out segments from between the membranes (these are called *suprêmes*). Drain the kumquats. Carefully place the citrus segments in the skillet (they are fragile) together with the kumquats. Bring to a boil and transfer immediately to a serving dish. Allow to cool and serve.

Here, we add dry hard apple cider and Calvados to this classic comfort food. All the heirloom apples are suitable, the Pippins in particular, of any color, size, or season.

French Toast

WITH APPLES

SERVES 4

1 vanilla bean
1 cup (250 ml) whole milk

CIDER BUTTER
1⅔ cups (400 ml) dry hard apple cider
2 tablespoons Calvados, or other apple brandy
6 teaspoons multi-floral honey, divided
3 tablespoons (40 g) lightly salted butter

6 apples
4 pinches cinnamon
1 stick (4 oz. / 120 g) unsalted butter, divided
4 slices sourdough country bread, 1-inch (2.5-cm) thick
3 eggs

Split the vanilla bean lengthwise and scrape out the seeds with a small knife. Pour the milk into a saucepan and add the vanilla bean and seeds. Bring to a boil and remove from the heat. Cover and allow to infuse.

FOR THE CIDER BUTTER
Pour the hard cider and Calvados into another saucepan and add 2 teaspoons of the honey. Set over medium heat and bring to a boil, then reduce by 90% to make a thick, syrupy consistency. Remove from the heat and whisk in the lightly salted butter. Set aside–it will need to be warm and runny when you are ready to serve.

Cut the apples into ¾-inch (1.5-cm) slices, then use a cookie cutter to make 1-inch- (2.5-cm-) diameter disks. Melt 5 tablespoons (3 oz. / 80 g) of the unsalted butter in a skillet over medium heat and lightly color the apple slices. Add the remaining honey and caramelize them lightly. Dust with the cinnamon and set aside.
Cut the slices of bread into halves and lightly moisten each piece with the vanilla-infused milk.
Beat the eggs. Melt the remaining unsalted butter in another skillet. As soon as it begins to foam, dip the bread slices in the beaten eggs. Ensure that the heat below the skillet is set to very low and cook the bread for 2 to 3 minutes on each side, just enough to color them.
Place the French toast on four plates and divide the apple slices over them. Drizzle with the warm cider butter and serve.

Use salted pork belly or pancetta for this recipe, or smoked bacon if you can't find either of those. When selecting your apples, go for Belle de Boskoop, Pippins, Braeburn, or Granny Smith. Should you prefer stronger notes of sweetness in the dish, opt for Golden Delicious, Juliet, Chantecler, or Gala.

Apple Carbonara

SERVES 4

4 slices salted pork belly or pancetta, each about ⅛ inch (3 to 4 mm) thick
1 large apple
Scant ½ cup (100 ml) dry hard apple cider
¾ cup (200 ml) crème fraîche or heavy cream
Fresh tagliatelle for 4
Salt and freshly ground pepper

Remove any rind from the pork and cut it into small squares. Crisp them in a skillet over medium-low slow heat.

Peel and dice the apple and add the dice to the skillet. Sauté the two ingredients together briefly, then pour in the hard cider. Continue cooking over medium heat until the liquid has evaporated.

Reduce the heat to low, stir in the crème fraîche, and cook for 5 minutes, until the sauce has thickened. Season very lightly with salt and grind in a generous amount of pepper.

Cook the tagliatelle according to instructions, combine with the sauce, and serve immediately.

Apple Carpaccio

AND APPLE FRITTERS

SERVES 2 TO 4

CARPACCIO
A little butter for the ovenproof dish
2 apples
2 ladlefuls* Apple Stock (see page 174)
*enough to cover the apples while they bake, approximately 1 cup (250 ml)

APPLE FRITTERS
1 cup (4½ oz. / 125 g) all-purpose flour, sifted
½ teaspoon (2.5 g) salt
2 teaspoons (8 g) sugar
Scant ¼ cup (50 ml) milk
3 tablespoons (50 g) unsalted butter, melted and divided into halves, plus 1 tablespoon (20 g) for the apples
2 eggs
⅓ cup (75 ml) blond ale
3 apples
2 tablespoons light brown sugar, plus a little extra for sprinkling (optional)
Oil for frying (a neutral oil such as grapeseed oil, sunflower oil, or Canola oil)

Accompany this apple carpaccio with apple fritters, and add a touch of luxury with a scoop of vanilla ice cream or a dollop of whipped cream. For the carpaccio, you'll need apples that hold up to cooking, like Golden Delicious, Granny Smith, Braeburn, Rubinette, or Chantecler), while sweet apples that soften are best for the fritters–think Golden Delicious, McIntosh, Gala, Chantecler, or Reinette Clochard. Of course, you can also simplify your life and use a single variety for both.

The carpaccio may be served hot, warm, or chilled, but the fritters should be served as soon as they have been fried and drained, so plan your timing accordingly.

Apple Carpaccio

AND APPLE FRITTERS

FOR THE CARPACCIO (MAKE AHEAD IF SERVED COLD)

Preheat the oven to 350°F (180°C). Butter an ovenproof dish. Peel the apples and slice them very finely. Arrange them in a rose pattern in the prepared dish. Pour in enough apple stock to just cover the slices. Bake for 45 minutes.

FOR THE APPLE FRITTERS

In the bowl of a stand mixer fitted with the paddle attachment, beat the flour, salt, sugar, milk, half of the melted butter, and the eggs until the mixture is completely smooth.

Replace the paddle attachment with the whisk and incorporate the beer. Strain the batter through a fine-mesh sieve into a bowl.

Whisk in the remaining melted butter; the batter should be completely smooth.

Allow to rest at room temperature for 30 minutes.

Peel the apples and cut them into quarters. In a skillet over medium-high heat, melt the butter and light brown sugar and sauté the apple quarters until golden all over.

Heat the oil to 330°F (165°C). Spear the apple quarters on the tines of a fork and dip them into the batter. Allow any excess to drip off and, working in batches if necessary, fry them for about 5 minutes, turning them over halfway through. When they are nicely colored all over, drain them on paper towels.

Serve them hot with the carpaccio, sprinkled, if you wish, with a little brown sugar.

The applesauce should have a good tang to it to offset the sweet creaminess of the cheesecake. Use Pippins, Belle de Boskoop, or heirloom varieties.

Apple Cheesecake

SERVES 6
OR MAKES ONE 7-INCH (18-CM) CAKE

COOKIE CRUMB BASE
24 butter biscuits, preferably
Petit-Lu (or other tea biscuits)
1½ sticks (6 oz. / 180 g)
unsalted butter, softened

CHEESECAKE FILLING
4 eggs
1 cup minus 3 tablespoons
(5½ oz. / 160 g) sugar
⅓ cup (1½ oz. / 40 g) all-purpose flour
1¾ lb. (800 g) triple-cream cream cheese,
32% butterfat (we recommend Kiri®)
1 cup (240 ml) whipping cream,
30 to 35% butterfat

CARAMEL APPLESAUCE
Scant ⅓ cup (2 oz. / 60 g) sugar
7½ oz. (210) Applesauce (see page 29)

CARAMELIZED CHOPPED ALMONDS
7 oz. (200 g) chopped almonds (about
1½ cups whole almonds, chopped)
¾ cup (3½ oz. / 100 g) confectioners' sugar

ASSEMBLY
Butter for pan

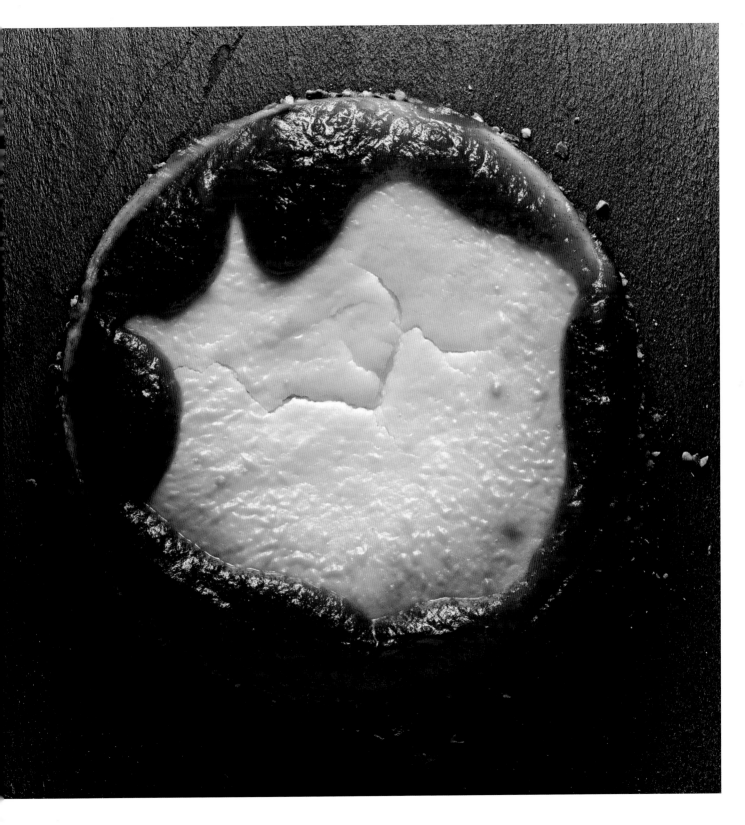

Apple Cheesecake

FOR THE CHEESECAKE FILLING
In a stand mixer with whisk attachment or using an electric beater, whisk the eggs and sugar until the mixture is pale and thick. Whisk in the flour, then the cream cheese, and lastly, the whipping cream. Set aside in the refrigerator.

FOR THE CARAMEL APPLESAUCE
Using the dry caramel method, cook the sugar to make a brown caramel. Cook the sugar to make a brown caramel. Immediately remove from the heat and deglaze it with the applesauce. Mix well and allow to cool.

FOR THE CARAMELIZED CHOPPED ALMONDS
In a saucepan over low heat, cook the chopped almonds with the confectioners' sugar, stirring until the almond pieces are coated in caramel. Carefully spread them over a sheet of wax paper and allow to cool.

FOR THE COOKIE CRUMB BASE
Finely crush the butter biscuits and combine them with the softened butter to form a paste. Shape the paste into a slightly flattened ball.

ASSEMBLE AND BAKE THE CHEESECAKE
Preheat the oven to 350°F (180°C). Butter a 7-inch (18-cm) springform or cake pan.
Using the palm of your hand, spread the crumb base evenly over the bottom of the pan. Pour in the cheesecake filling and bake for about 40 minutes, or more, depending on your oven.
Remove from the oven and allow to cool completely.
Spread the caramel applesauce evenly over the top of the cake, then gently press the chopped almonds around the sides.

To make a very clear jelly, use a clear artisanal apple juice. However, if you use unfiltered juice or apple purée, the jelly will not be quite as clear but it well be tastier. Of course, you can decorate it as you please: pick from what's in season and what you have at hand.

Green Apple Jelly

SERVES 4

1 teaspoon plus heaping ¼ teaspoon (0.2 oz. / 6 g) powdered gelatin
3 tablespoons (45 ml) very cold water
11½ oz. (325 g) apple purée, or 1⅓ cups (325 ml) artisanal apple juice
¾ teaspoon (3.5 ml) lime juice

VANILLA-SCENTED WHIPPED CREAM
¾ cup (200 ml) whipping cream, 30 to 35% butterfat, well chilled
Sugar to taste
Seeds of 1 vanilla bean

DECORATION
Wild strawberries
A few dollops of vanilla-scented whipping cream (see above)
Gooseberries
Small edible flowers, such as yellow pansies and cornflowers

Let the gelatin powder soak in the cold water for 10 minutes.
Heat the apple purée with the lime juice. Check with a thermometer: the final temperature should be 140°F (60°C).
Immediately stir in the gelatin and dissolve; divide the mixture between 4 bowls. Place in the refrigerator for at least 1 hour to set and chill.
Whisk the cream with the sugar and vanilla seeds until it is firm enough to be piped.
Spoon into a piping bag, ensure that no cream can leak, and place in the refrigerator until needed.
When the jelly has set, decorate the top of each bowl (see photo).

A classic applesauce, or compote as it is known in France, nicely flavored with vanilla. All apples work here, particularly those that soften well. And if you want to use several varieties, go ahead. When the applesauce is made, retrieve the vanilla beans and wash and dry them well. Reuse them, for example by placing them in a jar with sugar to make vanilla sugar.

Apple-y Sauce

MAKES ABOUT 2¼ LB. (1 KG)

1¾ lb. (800 g) apples, or apple pieces unused in another recipe
Scant ½ cup (100 ml) water
1 scant cup (6 oz. / 175 g) sugar
2 vanilla beans, split lengthwise and seeds scraped

Peel the apples and cut them into small pieces.

In a large saucepan, bring the water, sugar, and vanilla beans and seeds to a boil.

Add the apple pieces and simmer over low heat for 25 to 35 minutes, until the pieces are very soft and mushy.

Remove the vanilla beans and process the apples with an immersion blender, or in a food processor.

You will need a firm, very tart apple to accompany this risotto. We advise Granny Smith or King of the Pippins. Should you nevertheless prefer something else, go for a juicy, crunchy eating apple such as Gala, Fuji, Juliet, Pink Lady, or a fine Golden Delicious.

Lemon Risotto with Apples

SERVES 4

RISOTTO
Scant ½ cup (3 oz. / 85 g) round rice for risotto, such as arborio, carnarol, or vialone nano
2 cups (500 ml) whole milk
2 tablespoons (1 oz. / 25 g) sugar
1 vanilla bean, split lengthwise and seeds scraped
1 tablespoon (1/2 oz. / 15 g) butter
Grated zest of 1 lemon

ALMOND FOAM
Scant cup (100 ml) whole milk
1¾ oz. (50 g) almond paste, 60% almonds
Scant ½ cup (100 ml) whipping cream, 30 to 35% butterfat
0.4 oz. (12 g) soy lecithin

GARNISH
3 apples
Lemon juice to prevent the apples from browning

FOR THE RISOTTO

In a saucepan, cover the rice with water. Bring to a boil, reduce the heat to medium, and allow to boil for 2 minutes. Drain the rice, then transfer it to another saucepan. Pour in the milk and add the vanilla bean and seeds. Bring to a boil. Reduce the heat to very low and simmer for 15 to 17 minutes, until the rice has absorbed all of the milk. Remove from the heat, retrieve the vanilla bean, and stir in the butter and lemon zest. Transfer to a large, deep dish and allow to cool.

ALMOND FOAM (JUST BEFORE SERVING)

Bring the milk to a boil and pour it over the almond paste. Process with an immersion blender until perfectly smooth, then strain through a fine-mesh sieve into a saucepan. Stir in the whipping cream and lecithin and heat to between 105 and 115°F (40 to 45°C). Just before serving, emulsify the mixture using an immersion blender and scoop off the foam with a spoon.

TO PLATE

Using a mandoline with safety guard (or electric slicer), slice the apples thinly, and cut the slices into very thin sticks. Drizzle them with lemon juice so they do not brown. Drain the apple sticks and arrange them over the risotto. Top with the foam and serve.

If you prefer, you can make this recipe in six individual ramekins–this recipe works for both one large soufflé and six individual portions–you will just need to adjust the cooking time. You can make the applesauce with any cooking apple, such as Pippins, Chantecler, Golden Delicious, or Belle de Boskoop.

Apple Soufflé

FOR ONE 8-INCH (20-CM) SOUFFLÉ DISH

Softened butter and sugar for the soufflé dish
1½ tablespoons (15 g) cornstarch
3 tablespoons (45 ml) artisanal apple juice, divided
3 tablespoons (1½ oz. / 45 g) applesauce
2 teaspoons (10 ml) Calvados or other apple brandy
⅔ cup (5 oz. / 140 g) egg whites, or just under 5 egg whites
1 pinch salt
¼ cup plus 1 teaspoon (2 oz. / 55 g) sugar, divided
Confectioners' sugar for decoration

SPECIAL EQUIPMENT
An apple-shaped stencil for decoration

Preheat the oven to 480°F (250°C) using the convection setting, if you have one.

Generously butter the soufflé mold and dust the mold with sugar. Dissolve the cornstarch in a little of the apple juice and place in a small saucepan. Add the remaining apple juice and the applesauce and bring to a boil. Reduce the heat to low and stir in the cornstarch-apple juice mixture. Stir constantly until the mixture thickens–this is like making pastry cream. Remove from the heat, stir in the Calvados, and set aside. Whisk the egg whites in a stand mixer with the whisk attachment at low speed with the salt and a little of the sugar. When the whites are frothy, add the remaining sugar and finish whisking at high speed to the soft peak stage.

Carefully fold the whisked egg whites into the thickened applesauce-apple juice mixture, taking care not to deflate the whites. Pour the batter into the soufflé dish. To ensure that there are no large air bubbles, lightly rap the dish on a work surface. Smooth the top of the soufflé and run your finger around the top of the rim.

Place in the oven and bake for 6 minutes (about 4 minutes if you are making smaller, individual soufflés), until nicely risen with a light crust on the top.

Immediately, place the stencil over the top and dust with the confectioners' sugar. Serve immediately.

Apple Jelly

MAKES ABOUT 1 LB. 2 OZ. (500 G) FOR TWO JARS

2¼ lb. (1 kg) juicy, crisp, tart apples (preferably organic, from a farmers' market)
1 juicy unwaxed lemon
1 bottle (3 cups / 750 ml) dry hard apple cider, plus 1 cup (250 ml) water
or 4 cups (1 liter) water
Sugar–the amount depends on how much juice you have
(Allow 1¼ cups (9 oz. / 250 g) for every 2 cups (500 ml) of juice)
A little Calvados or other apple brandy (optional)

The lovely orange-hued jelly shown here has been prepared using heirloom varieties from farms in Normandy, notably the Bailleul. It has everything one could wish for: abundant juice, pectin, and tartness. But any tangy, juicy apple will work well. Go for Rubinettes, Pippins, or Granny Smiths (as long as you avoid the supermarket versions). Using this recipe as a base, you can make variations by adding a quince (it should be washed, brushed, and quartered–use the skin and seeds) or spicing it up with a cinnamon stick or vanilla bean.

Apple Jelly

Cut the apples into quarters. Place them in a pot.

Halve the lemon and squeeze the juice, keeping the pulp and seeds. Add the juice, pulp, and seeds to the pot.

Cover with the hard cider and water and bring to a boil over low heat, keeping an eye on the pot–the liquid should not overflow.

Cover the pot with the lid and simmer over very low heat for 1 hour; this will ensure that the flavors and pectin of the fruit are all exuded.

Place a large fine-mesh sieve over a large bowl. Line it with two layers of cheesecloth.

Carefully pour the contents of the pot into the sieve and allow to drain for at least 3 hours, or overnight if possible. Do not apply any pressure to the fruit.

Sterilize the jars and their lids: Clean them and place them in a 250°F (120°C) oven for 1 hour.

When the apples and lemons render no more juice, measure the amount of juice obtained.

Measure 1¼ cups (9 oz. / 250 g) sugar for every 2 cups of juice.

Combine the sugar and juice in a saucepan, which may be copper, enamel, or steel, but not aluminum. Place over low heat and stir gently to dissolve the sugar.

Place a porcelain saucer in the freezer: you will need it to test whether the jelly has set.

When the sugar has dissolved, bring the syrup to a boil. (If you are incorporating spices, add them soon after boiling point is reached.)

Allow to boil until the jelly sets, checking for doneness every 5 minutes when you think it might be ready. To do this, place a drop of syrup on the cold saucer. If it runs, this means it is has not set. Return the saucer to the freezer.

As soon as the drop of jelly sets on immediate contact with the cold saucer and wrinkles when you brush your finger over it, remove the saucepan from the heat and pour the preparation into the jars.

Cover the jars with sheets of paper towel and allow to cool until the following day.

In order to extend the shelf life of your jelly, cut out disks of wax paper slightly smaller than the neck of the jars, dip them in Calvados, and press them down lightly onto the surface of the jelly, without creating any air bubbles.

Seal the jars. They can now be kept for at least a year in a cool, dark place.

When the jars are opened, they will keep for about 2 months, refrigerated.

Select firm apples that are slightly tangy, such as any of the Pippins, Chantecler, and Belle de Boskoop. Look for honeycomb at specialized honey stores or at Middle Eastern grocery stores, or buy online.

Roasted Apples with Honey

SERVES 4

6 medium apples or 10 small apples
2 tablespoons (30 g) unsalted butter, plus extra for the dish
3 tablespoons (50 g) lightly salted butter
1¾ oz. (50 g) honeycomb
or
5 heaping tablespoons flavorful honey

Preheat the oven to 400°F (200°C). Butter an appropriately sized ovenproof dish.

Using a small, pointed knife, score the skin of each apple in a spiral around its entire circumference.

Arrange the apples in the dish. Dot the two types of butter evenly around the dish. Dice the honeycomb and divide the cubes evenly among the apples.

Bake for 50 minutes to 1 hour, drizzling the apples from time to time with the juices in the pan.

Serve warm or chilled.

The tangy freshness of the Granny Smith, transformed into sorbet, will cool you down on a hot summer's day. There's no reason not to enjoy it in winter when the green fruit are freshly available–a dessert for all seasons. Keep in mind that the sorbet preparation requires a long chilling period before it is churned.

Iced Apple

SERVES 6

APPLE SORBET
2 lb. 10 oz. (1.2 kg) Granny Smith apples
Scant ¼ cup (50 ml) lemon juice
1 cup (250 ml) water
Scant ⅔ cup (4 oz. / 120 g) sugar
3½ oz. (100 g) atomized glucose (powder form)
0.7 oz. (20 g) trimoline (invert sugar)

6 Granny Smith apples
Juice of 1 lemon

APPLE SORBET

A day ahead, core the Granny Smith apples. Ensure that there are no seeds or any parts of the core remaining with the flesh. Process it in a juicer to make 4 cups (1 liter) of apple pulp. Stir in the lemon juice.
In a saucepan, combine the water, sugar, atomized glucose, and trimoline and bring to a boil.
Remove from the heat and allow to cool to 140°F (60°C). Add the apple pulp to the cooling mixture and process with an immersion blender. Cover with a lid or plastic wrap and place in the refrigerator to chill for 12 hours.

PREPARE THE ICED APPLES

Slice them across the top to make "hats" and, using a small scoop or melon baller, scoop out the flesh, keeping the skin intact. Rub lemon juice over the remaining flesh and that of the "hat" to prevent it from browning. Place the hollowed apples in the freezer.

ASSEMBLE THE SORBET AND FILL THE APPLES

Process the sorbet preparation thoroughly with the immersion blender on removing it from the refrigerator and churn, following the directions on your ice cream maker.
Fill the hollowed apples, top with the hat, and return to the freezer until ready to serve.

A sophisticated dessert encased in a globe of crisp blown sugar made to look like Granny Smiths, this is one of the most famous creations of Christelle Brua, head pastry chef at triple-Michelin–starred Le Pré Catelan, Paris, whose chef, Frédéric Anton, inspired her to revisit the candy apples of carnivals. Christelle was kind enough to send us her recipe to be included in this book.

Souffléed Crisp Apple

WITH CARAMBAR® ICE CREAM, HARD CIDER, AND POPPING SUGAR

SERVES 4

CARAMBAR® ICE CREAM
¾ cup (180 ml) whole milk
¾ cup (180 ml) whipping cream, 30 to 35% butterfat
4 Carambar® candies (chewy French caramel candies)
4 egg yolks
Scant ½ cup (3 oz. / 80 g) sugar

BLOWN SUGAR GLOBE
5½ oz. (160 g) sugar cubes
⅓ cup (80 ml) water
1¾ oz. (50 g) glucose syrup
0. 04 oz. (1 g) green food coloring

LIGHT CREAM WITH APPLE
1 vanilla bean
Scant ¾ cup (170 ml) whole milk
2 egg yolks
¼ cup (1¾ oz. / 50 g) sugar
1 tablespoon (0.28 oz. / 8 g) flour
2½ teaspoons (0.28 oz. / 8 g) custard powder or cornstarch

1 teaspoon (4 g) butter
⅓ cup (80 ml) whipping cream, 30 to 35% butterfat, well chilled
3 teaspoons (0.28 oz. / 8 g) confectioners' sugar
0.35 oz. (10 g) very finely diced Granny Smith apple (*brunoise*)

CIDER FOAM
1 sheet (2 g) gelatin
1⅔ cups (400 ml) dry hard cider
3½ tablespoons (1½ oz. / 40 g) sugar
¾ cup (180 ml) whipping cream, 30 to 35% butterfat

FOR DECORATION
1½ oz. (40 g) small shards of shortcrust pastry
1½ oz. (40 g) caramelized puffed rice
¾ oz. (20 g) popping sugar
4 disks of Genovese sponge, each 1¼ inches (3 cm)
4 edible silver leaves
Scant ½ cup (100 ml) apple syrup
Edible silver powder for dusting

SPECIAL EQUIPMENT
Sugar lamp
Sugar pump
Siphon with 3 gas cartridges (see pg. 187)
Nozzle

Souffléed Crisp Apple

WITH CARAMBAR® ICE CREAM, HARD CIDER, AND POPPING SUGAR

FOR THE CARAMBAR® ICE CREAM

Bring the milk and cream to a boil. Add the Carambar® candies and allow them to melt completely. Whisk the egg yolks with the sugar until the mixture is pale, then carefully pour the milk-cream liquid over the egg-sugar mixture, whisking constantly. Return to the heat and cook, stirring constantly, until the mixture reaches 181°F (83°C)–it should coat the back of a spoon at this stage. Remove from the heat, process the ice cream in an ice cream maker according to manufacturer's instructions, and place in the freezer.

FOR THE BLOWN SUGAR GLOBE

Bring the sugar and water to a boil, skimming off any scum. Add the glucose, then heat to 310°F (155°C). Incorporate the green food coloring and spread the sugar mixture over a silicone baking mat. Working with a spatula, turn and stir it until it is smooth. Take a piece and keep it warm under a sugar lamp (A sugar lamp is useful for keeping sugar at the right temp to be worked. It is available at kitchen supply stores. A very powerful lightbulb will also do the trick). Using a sugar pump, make a globe the size of an apple. Set aside, protected from any moisture. Repeat to make 3 more globes.

FOR THE LIGHT CREAM (A PASTRY CREAM COMBINED WITH CHANTILLY CREAM)

Split the vanilla bean lengthwise and scrape out the seeds with a small knife. Pour the milk into a saucepan, add the vanilla bean and seeds, and bring to a boil. Remove from the heat and cover the saucepan.

Whisk the egg yolks with the sugar until the mixture is pale. Whisk in the flour and custard powder. Remove the vanilla bean from the milk and carefully pour the milk over the yolk-sugar mixture, whisking continuously. Return to low heat, stirring constantly until the liquid thickens. Transfer the pastry cream to a mixing bowl, whisk in the butter, cover with plastic wrap, and allow to cool completely.

Make the apple–Chantilly cream: whisk the whipping cream with the confectioners' sugar, then carefully stir in the finely diced apple. Combine the pastry cream with the apple–Chantilly cream and place in the refrigerator.

FOR THE CIDER FOAM

Soak the gelatin sheet in very cold water for 10 minutes. Bring the hard cider to a boil, then add the sugar and the cream. Bring to a boil once again, drain the gelatin, and stir it in. Allow to cool, pour into a siphon, and fit the siphon with 3 gas cartridges.

TO ASSEMBLE AND PLATE

Place a globe of sugar in front of you with the opening facing upward. Insert the cider foam, add some of the shards of shortcrust pastry, puffed rice, and popping sugar. Place a scoop of Carambar® ice cream inside. Cover with the light cream, then close up the globe with a disk of Genovese sponge. Turn upside down so that the globe rests on the sponge disk in the center of the plate. Top with the silver leaf. Combine a little of the apple syrup with the silver powder. Place the mixture into a paper cone and dot the plates with it, surrounding the apple globe. Serve immediately.

Finest-quality Golden Delicious or Chantecler will give firmness, crunch, and notes of vanilla to these wraps, inspired by the apple strudel. Choose apples that have a good size.

Apple Wrap

STRUDEL STYLE

SERVES 4

3 tablespoons (1¾ oz. / 50 g) lightly salted butter, plus extra for the pan
4 large apples
3 tablespoons multi-floral honey
Juice of 2 oranges
⅔ cup (3½ oz. / 100 g) sultanas
1 teaspoon cinnamon
1 lb. 2 oz. (500 g) Puff Pastry (see page 58) or store-bought
1 egg, lightly beaten, for the egg wash
1 cup (3½ oz. / 100 g) ground almonds

SPECIAL EQUIPMENT
A "tuile" baking tray or baguette mold (with channels)

Make the filling: Heat the butter over low heat until it browns (this is called *beurre noisette*, hazelnut butter). Remove from the heat and pour it into a small nonstick pan.

Peel and cut the apples into a small dice. Sauté them in the browned butter over medium heat for 2 minutes. Lower the heat and continue cooking gently until they are a nice golden color.

Stir in the honey and allow to caramelize, then deglaze with the orange juice. Stir in the sultanas. Reduce for about 10 minutes so the filling can absorb the orange flavor. Transfer to a colander to drain and cool. Sprinkle with the cinnamon.

Roll the puff pastry into a 16 by 20-inch (40 by 52-cm) rectangle. Brush the entire surface with the egg wash and cut it into four strips each 5 by 16 inches (13 by 40 cm). Spread the apple-raisin mixture over them. Sprinkle with the ground almonds and roll the strips up neatly. Brush again with the egg wash and place in the refrigerator to chill for 1 hour.

Preheat the oven to 350°F (180°C). Butter a tuile pan and place the wraps in the hollows. (If you don't have a tuile pan, shape some sturdy aluminum foil around the wraps to hold them in shape.) Brush again with the egg wash. Bake for 30 to 40 minutes, until heated through and golden on the outside.

Allow to cool and cut each wrap at an angle into two. Serve upright on plates.

Layered Caramel Chantilly Cream, Flambéed Apples, and Blackberries

SERVES 4

CARAMEL CHANTILLY CREAM
3 sheets (6 g) gelatin
2½ cups (600 ml) whipping cream, 35% butterfat
Scant cup (6 oz. / 180 g) sugar
1 pinch fleur de sel or other flaky salt

PAN-FRIED APPLES
4 apples
3 tablespoons (1¾ oz. / 50 g) lightly salted butter
3 tablespoons plus 1 teaspoon (1 oz. / 30 g) light brown sugar
Scant ¼ cup (50 ml) Calvados or other apple brandy

CRÊPES, TORTILLA STYLE
2 crêpes (make your usual recipe, or use store-bought crêpes)
Softened butter
Brown sugar to taste
Grated zest of 1 unwaxed lemon

GARNISH
4 oz. (125 g) blackberries
4 oz. (125 g) blueberries
Borage flowers

SPECIAL EQUIPMENT
A "tuile" baking tray or baguette mold (with channels)
Siphon with 2 gas cartridges (see pg. 187)
Plain nozzle

For this recipe, all the Pippins and heirloom varieties are recommended—make sure they are full of flavor. If you don't have a "tuile" baking tray, simply drape the baked crêpes over a rolling pin or clean bottle as soon as you remove them from the oven to curve them.

FOR THE CARAMEL CHANTILLY CREAM
Soften the gelatin in a bowl of cold water for 10 minutes. Pour the cream into a saucepan over medium heat and bring to a simmer. Remove from the heat immediately.

Using the dry caramel method (p. 186), cook the sugar to make a brown caramel. Remove from the heat, add the salt, and carefully deglaze with the hot cream–the hot caramel might spatter. When the caramel has dissolved in the cream, drain the water from the gelatin and stir it in until completely dissolved. Cover and place in the refrigerator to chill for at least 3 hours–it must be very cold when you transfer it into the siphon.

PAN-FRIED APPLES
Peel the apples and cut them into cubes. Place the butter and brown sugar in a skillet and cook over medium heat until they form a light caramel. Stir in the apple cubes, reduce the heat to low, and cook until lightly colored. Pour in the Calvados and carefully flambé the contents of the skillet. Allow to cool completely and chill slightly (they will be placed atop the chilled cream).

FOR THE CRÊPES, TORTILLA STYLE
Preheat the oven to 340°F (170°C).
Brush the crêpes with the softened butter and sprinkle them with the brown sugar and lemon zest. Cut them into triangles and place in the "tuile" mold. Bake for 10 minutes and allow to cool in the mold. (If you don't have a "tuile" mold to shape the crêpes, you can simply bake them flat.)

TO ASSEMBLE AND SERVE
Transfer the caramel cream to a siphon fitted with a plain nozzle. Insert 2 gas cartridges and half-fill the serving dish. Arrange the apple pieces over the surface of the cream, setting aside a few for decoration. Pipe dollops of cream over the apple layer, covering it completely. Stand the tortilla-style crêpes in the cream, then arrange the blueberries, blackcurrants, and remaining apple pieces. Decorate with the borage flowers.

We recommend Belle de Boskoop or Chantecler for this unusual, sweet take on the savory side dish.

Apple Gratin Dauphinois

SERVES 6

2¼ lb. (1 kg) apples
3 vanilla beans
¾ cup (200 ml) whole milk
1¼ cups (300 ml) whipping cream
1 cinnamon stick
2 handfuls light brown sugar
1 tablespoon plus 1 teaspoon (20 g) unsalted butter

Peel the apples, ensuring they remain whole and reserving the skin. With an apple corer, remove the cores and slice the apples into thin rounds.

Split the vanilla beans lengthwise and scrape out the seeds.

Pour the milk and cream into a saucepan. Add the cinnamon stick, 1 handful of the brown sugar, 2 handfuls of apple skins, and the vanilla beans and seeds. Place over medium heat and bring gently to a boil. At the first sign of boiling, reduce the heat to low and cover with the lid. Simmer very gently for 30 minutes to infuse all the flavors. Strain the liquid through a fine mesh sieve into a bowl or jug.

Preheat the oven to 400°F (200°C). Arrange the apple rounds in an ovenproof dish, preferably round or oval, making several layers of a rose pattern.

Pour the vanilla-scented cream over the apples, then dot small knobs of butter over the top. Sprinkle with the remaining handful of brown sugar. Bake for 45 minutes to 1 hour, depending on your oven and how the apples color.

To achieve the right texture of this marmalade, you will need firm apples with flesh that is transparent and crunchy. Rubinette is the ideal variety, with Royal Gala a close second. If you are lucky enough to stumble on Calville Rouge d'Hiver, Patte-de-Loup, or Juliet–organic, of course–do give them a try. The photo opposite illustrates the best serving suggestion: thick slices of toasted sourdough bread smeared with old-fashioned cream that comes straight from the farm.

Apple Marmalade

MAKES ABOUT 2¼ LB. (1 KG) MARMALADE

2¼ lb. (1 kg) Royal Gala apples
2½ cups (1 lb. 2 oz. / 500 g) sugar
1 cinnamon stick
Juice of 1 lemon

TO SERVE
Country bread, sourdough bread, or granola loaf
Thick farm cream

Peel the apples and use a corer to remove the cores. Cut the flesh into small pieces and place them in a heavy-bottomed saucepan. Add the sugar, cinnamon stick, and lemon juice.

Place over low heat, stirring from time to time, for 10 minutes to ensure that the sugar is completely dissolved. Then increase the heat to medium and cook for 1 hour 30 minutes, stirring regularly with a wooden spoon so that the apple pieces don't stick to the bottom of the saucepan. The apple pieces should be transparent and the mixture, syrupy.

Transfer the marmalade to a large mixing bowl and cover it with a clean cloth. Place in the refrigerator to cool overnight, and store in the refrigerator.

New Zealanders and Australians both claim to have created the pavlova. According to New Zealanders, the dessert was first made in 1926 in Wellington, and according to Australians, it first appeared in 1935 in Perth. There is agreement on one matter: It was created as a tribute to Russian ballerina Anna Pavlova. The now well-known classic dessert comprises a meringue with a crisp crust and chewy interior, topped with fruit and whipped cream, sometimes even ice cream. Here is our take on a pavlova, one that has not fallen too far from the original tree. Choose varieties from those recommended for the Apple Upside-Down Tartlets (page 110), which is the basis for this recipe.

Some important advice: A few hours before you begin, place a mixing bowl in the freezer. It will be required for the custard (*crème anglaise*). The custard, as well as the caramel whipped cream, should be made at least three hours ahead so that they both have time to chill before serving.

Apple-Caramel Pavlova

SERVES 6

6 apple domes (see page 110) to make a day ahead (without the puff pastry) in 1½-inch (4-cm) hemispherical silicone molds

CARAMEL CUSTARD
1½ cups (375 ml) whole milk
⅓ cup (75 ml) whipping cream, 30 to 35% butterfat
⅓ cup (2¼ oz. / 65 g) sugar
6 egg yolks
Heaping ½ teaspoon (3 g) salt

CARAMEL CHANTILLY CREAM
3 sheets (6 g) gelatin
2½ cups (600 ml) whipping cream, 35% butterfat
Scant cup (6 oz. / 180 g) sugar
1 pinch fleur de sel or other flaky salt

MERINGUE
3 egg whites
1 pinch salt
Scant ½ cup (3 oz. / 80 g) sugar
⅔ cup (3 oz. / 80 g) confectioners' sugar, sifted
1 handful chopped roasted almonds

Apple-Caramel Pavlova

FOR THE CARAMEL CUSTARD

Bring the milk and cream to a simmer. Using the dry caramel method, cook the sugar to make a brown caramel. Immediately remove from the heat and carefully pour in the milk-cream mixture to deglaze—the hot caramel might spatter. Stir well to combine.

In a mixing bowl, whisk the egg yolks and carefully incorporate them into the caramel mixture. (It is a good idea to first pour some of the warm liquid into the whisked yolks, combine the two, and then return the mixture to the hot liquid in the saucepan.) Place the saucepan over low heat and, stirring constantly, bring to 185°F (85°C) if you have a thermometer, or until the custard coats the back of the spoon. Do not cook the custard any further. Pour it into the well-chilled bowl and process with an immersion blender. Place in the refrigerator to chill for at least 3 hours.

FOR THE CARAMEL CHANTILLY CREAM

Soften the gelatin in a bowl of cold water for 10 minutes. Pour the cream into a saucepan over medium heat and bring to a simmer. Remove from the heat immediately.

Using the dry caramel method (see p. 186), cook the sugar to make a brown caramel. Remove from the heat, add the salt, and carefully deglaze with the hot cream—the hot caramel might spatter. When the caramel has dissolved in the cream, drain the water from the gelatin and stir it in until completely dissolved. Cover and place in the refrigerator to chill for at least 3 hours before you whisk it.

FOR THE MERINGUE

Preheat the oven to 265°F (130°C). Line a baking sheet with parchment paper.

Using an electric beater, whisk the egg whites with the pinch of salt, starting at low speed. When the egg whites become frothy, increase the speed. In three additions, add the sugar, whisking constantly. As soon as the sugar has been incorporated, stop working with the beater and use a flexible spatula to fold in the confectioners' sugar.

Spoon the meringue into a pastry bag fitted with a plain ⅓-inch (7-mm) tip. Pipe out six 2¾-inch (7-cm) rings of meringue. Inside each ring, pipe a spiral of meringue. Pipe another layer of meringue over the ring—this makes a rim for the pavlova and allows the caramel Chantilly cream to be held in place. Sprinkle with some of the chopped almonds, reserving a few for decoration.

Bake for about 15 minutes; the pavlova should remain soft inside. Transfer to a rack to cool and store, if necessary, in a dry place.

TO ASSEMBLE (TEN MINUTES BEFORE SERVING, NO EARLIER, SO THAT THE MERINGUE DOESN'T SOFTEN)

Whisk the caramel-flavored cream until it reaches a Chantilly texture. Place a meringue in the center of each plate and fill the center with the caramel Chantilly cream. Cover with an apple dome and pour the caramel custard around the pavlova. Scatter with chopped roasted almonds and serve.

Liquid

This toddy can also be attractively presented in glasses garnished with thin slices of unpeeled, red-skinned apples. Should you prefer an even more pronounced taste of apple, use a vegetable peeler to remove the skin of one or two flavorful red apples and stir it in.

Spiced Apple Toddy

WITH THANKS TO LAURENT JEANNIN

SERVES 2

¾ cup (200 ml) dry hard apple cider
Scant ¼ cup (50 ml) lime juice
⅓ cup (75 ml) dark rum
Generous ⅓ cup (3 oz. / 80 g) brown sugar
½ cinnamon stick
½ vanilla bean
¼ clove
2 oz. (50 g) fresh ginger, thinly sliced
Zest of 1 lime, cut into strips
2 pinches freshly grated nutmeg

Combine all the ingredients in a saucepan and bring to a boil. Remove from the heat, cover with the lid, and leave to infuse for 30 minutes.
Pour into glasses or mugs and serve.

In 1975, the legendary chef Paul Bocuse created a soup for then President Valéry Giscard d'Estaing. It is now famously known as the Soupe VGE: a chicken broth richly flavored with black truffles that contains both chicken breast and foie gras, sealed by a puff pastry top. Once the soup bowls are covered with the pastry, they are baked in the oven to emerge with a crisp, golden dome. For this fruity interpretation, use firm, tangy, well-flavored apples–medium-sized are best. All the Pippins will work well, in particular the Reinette Clochard and the King of Pippins.

Apple Soup under a Pastry Crust

INSPIRED BY PAUL BOCUSE

SERVES 4

4 Pippin apples
1 vanilla bean
1 strip orange zest
1 strip lemon zest
3 cups (750 ml) apple stock (see page 174)
4 oz. (125 g) fresh raspberries
4 tablespoons Pommeau de Normandie liqueur (a blend of Calvados and fresh artisanal apple juice, with an alcohol content of 16 to 18%), or 2 tablespoons of Calvados (apple brandy)
1 lb. 2 oz. (500 g) homemade puff pastry (see page 58) or store-bought
1 egg yolk for the egg wash

SPECIAL EQUIPMENT

Four thick, white porcelain onion soup bowls (traditional "lion-head" bowls if possible), or any other ovenproof ceramic bowls, with a diameter of 5 inches (13 cm).

Peel and core the apples and cut them into ¾-inch (2-cm) cubes.

Split the vanilla bean lengthwise and scrape out the seeds.

In a pot or large saucepan, combine the apple cubes, vanilla bean and seeds, and citrus zests. Pour in the apple stock and bring to a boil. Reduce the heat to low, cover with the lid, and simmer gently for 5 minutes. The apple cubes should be lightly poached, not cooked through.

Remove from the heat and drain, reserving the cooking liquid. Discard the vanilla bean (when rinsed and dried, it can be used to flavor a jar of sugar) and zests. Allow to cool to room temperature.

Preheat the oven to 430°F (220°C).

Divide the apple cubes and raspberries among the soup bowls.

Stir the Pommeau into the reserved cooking liquid and divide among the four bowls.

Roll the puff pastry out and cut out 4 disks with a diameter slightly larger than that of the bowls. Place the disks over the bowls and press down firmly around the rims to seal the contents in: the pastry should form an airtight "lid."

Lightly beat the egg yolk with a few drops of water and brush over the puff pastry. If you wish, you may decorate the pastry with the tip of a knife. Bake for 18 to 20 minutes, until golden and well risen.

Serve immediately, allowing each guest to break their puff pastry lid at the table.

Fruit soups, including those made with apples, plums, and cherries, are very popular in Hungary. Hot or chilled, they are served as a starter rather than as a dessert. For this recipe, we recommend firm, very tangy apples, such as Belle de Boskoop, Braeburn, Reinette Grise du Canada (also known as Pomme Gris or Pomme Grise), or Granny Smith. The more flavorful the apples, the tastier this soup will be—we recommend you select an heirloom variety if possible.

Hungarian Apple Soup

ALMA LEVES

SERVES 4

6 tangy apples
4 tablespoons (2 oz. / 60 g) lightly salted butter
4 tablespoons sugar
½ tablespoon cinnamon
¾ cup (200 ml) crème fraîche or heavy cream
2 tablespoons flour
Lemon juice for seasoning
Zest of 1 lemon and/or 1 orange

Peel and core the apples and cut them into small, even cubes. Heat the butter in a large saucepan or pot over medium heat with the sugar and cinnamon and sauté the apple cubes. Continue cooking until the liquid has evaporated and the apple cubes are lightly caramelized. Pour in 2¾ cups (700 ml) water, bring to a boil, and allow to simmer for 15 minutes.

In the meantime, whisk the cream, flour, and ⅓ cup (70 ml) water in a mixing bowl. When the apples are cooked, carefully whisk this mixture into the saucepan with the apples. Return to low heat and, stirring constantly, bring back to a simmer. Remove from the heat and allow to cool. Adjust the seasoning by adding lemon juice if necessary. Cover the saucepan with the lid and chill in the refrigerator for at least 2 hours if you wish to serve the soup cold. You can also serve it hot.

Ladle the soup into bowls and grate lemon or orange zest over each one.

Trou Normand

SERVES 4

APPLE SORBET
1 lb. 5 oz. (600 g) Pink Lady apples
2 tablespoons (25 ml) lemon juice
½ cup (125 ml) water
Scant ⅓ cup (2 oz. / 60 g) sugar
1.76 oz. (50 g) atomized glucose (also known as glucose powder)
0.35 oz. (10 g) trimoline (liquid invert sugar)

NOUGATINE
3½ oz. (100 g) sliced almonds (about 1 cup)
Neutral oil for the work surface and rolling pin
Scant ⅓ cup (3½ oz. / 100 g) glucose syrup
⅔ cup (4½ oz. / 125 g) sugar

PAN-FRIED APPLES
3 apples (see introduction to the recipe)
4 tablespoons (2 oz. / 60 g) unsalted butter
2 tablespoons (1 oz. / 25 g) light brown sugar

TO SERVE
1 Granny Smith apple
1¼ cups (300 ml) apple stock (see page 174)
2 tablespoons (30 ml) Calvados (or other apple brandy)

Select Pippins or any other sweet variety with firm flesh for the pan-fried apples. We recommend Golden Delicious (but only the finest of this variety), Chantecler, Cox Orange, or Jonagold. If you'd like the flavors of Normandy to be even more pronounced, increase the amount of Calvados slightly. (We'll keep your secret.)

Be sure to make the apple stock and the preparation for the sorbet 24 hours ahead. Note that the sorbet calls for certain ingredients that are best weighed accurately. Making the nougatine also calls for careful timing.

FOR THE APPLE SORBET PREPARATION

A day ahead, core the apples and juice them; you should have 2 cups (500 ml) of juice. Stir in the lemon juice.

In a saucepan, combine the water, sugar, atomized glucose, and trimoline and bring to a boil. Remove from the heat and allow to cool to 140°F (60°C). Pour in the apple juice and process with an immersion blender. Transfer to a bowl if necessary, cover, and place in the refrigerator to chill for at least 12 hours.

FOR THE NOUGATINE

The sliced almonds must be hot when incorporated into the caramel, so plan carefully.

Preheat the oven to 320°F (160°C). Lightly oil a clean work surface, as well as a rolling pin.

Spread the sliced almonds over a baking sheet and roast them for 5 to 7 minutes while you prepare the caramel–but don't forget to remove them from the oven in time! They should be only very lightly colored. Do not switch off the oven, as you may need it a few minutes later.

While the almonds are roasting, heat the glucose in a saucepan over low heat until it liquefies. Gradually add the sugar and continue cooking until the mixture forms a nice brown caramel. Carefully stir in the still-hot almonds. When they are evenly distributed, pour the mixture over the prepared work surface and roll it out as thinly as possible. If the mixture becomes too hard, transfer it carefully to a baking sheet lined with wax paper or a silicone baking mat and return it to the oven for the few minutes it takes to soften again, then roll it out very thinly.

Using a 2-inch (5-cm) cookie cutter, cut out 4 rounds of nougatine. Allow them to cool and store in an airtight container until needed.

FOR THE PAN-FRIED APPLES

Peel and core the apples and cut them into ½-inch (1.5-cm) dice. Melt the butter in a skillet and lightly color the apple cubes. Sprinkle them with the light brown sugar and allow to caramelize slightly.

TO FINISH AND PLATE

Following the directions for your ice cream maker, churn the sorbet preparation.

In the meanwhile, wash the Granny Smith apple and cut it into a very small dice (a *brunoise*). Combine the apple stock and Calvados.

Divide the pan-fried apples among four dessert bowls. Pour a little of the liquid over each. Then arrange the diced Granny Smith evenly over the first apple layer. Place the bowls in the refrigerator to chill for 15 minutes. Just before serving, add a scoop of sorbet and a disk of nougatine.

This is a decoction made with fruit peels–mainly apple peel–and spices that is used like a stock or broth. You can select any variety of apple, and while some recipes in this book call for apple stock, you can use it many other ways: as a drink on its own, hot or cold, just like an herbal brew; as an ingredient in cocktails or as part of an infusion; as a base for a jelly or glaze with gelatin or agar agar powder; or in a dessert, sorbet, or ice cream. One thing is essential: the fruit must all be organic because the peels are used. Of course, there will be a multitude of uses in other recipes for the flesh of all the fruit.

Apple Stock

MAKES 5 CUPS (1.25 LITERS) STOCK

4 organic apples of any variety
1 organic pineapple
1 organic orange
1 organic lemon
6 cups (1.5 liters) water
3⅔ cups (1½ lb. / 700 g) sugar
2 licorice root sticks
1 stick lemon grass
3 vanilla beans, preferably Madagascar vanilla, split lengthwise and seeds scraped
1 star anise

Carefully wash the apples and pineapple. Using a very sharp knife, remove the skins.

Wash the orange and lemon and squeeze them. Reserve the juice and the peel.

Pour the water into a pot, add the sugar, and bring gently to a boil. Add the licorice root sticks, lemon grass, vanilla beans and seeds, star anise, citrus juice and peel, and apple and pineapple skins.

Bring to a boil over medium-high heat and then reduce the heat to low. Half cover the pot with a lid and simmer gently for 1 hour 30 minutes. Remove from the heat and allow to cool. Strain the liquid through a fine-mesh sieve into a container that has an airtight lid, or into a bottle that can be tightly closed.

Store in the refrigerator, where it will keep for up to two weeks.

Index

Index of Recipes by Chapter

Index of Recipes by Category

Christophe Adam

By the time he was sixteen years old, Christophe Adam knew that he would be a pastry chef. Born in Brittany, in the Cornouaille area, he received his basic training at the Legrand pastry store in the town of Quimper as soon as he had finished school. Two years later, he was in London, in the pastry kitchen of the triple-Michelin-starred Gavroche restaurant. He had set out on his quest to master his niche of refined gastronomy.

Back in Paris, he worked at the luxurious Hôtel de Crillon with Christophe Felder, honing his art and becoming ever more demanding of himself. After a three-year stint with Laurent Jeannin, one of France's most talented pastry chefs, he continued on to the Beau-Rivage Palace in Lausanne to work as its pastry chef. In December 1996 Adam moved to Fauchon, the Paris food emporium. There, he began asserting his individual style, his energy and creativity taking him to the position of head pastry chef in 2001. He overhauled the classic éclair, transforming it in a multitude of shapes and flavors. When Fauchon opened its bakery in 2007, he was in the vanguard of the creation of le snacking chic: upmarket, easy-to-eat nibbles for people on the go. With Adam overseeing operations, Fauchon opened a string of stores in Monaco, Bordeaux, New York, Moscow, Beijing, Dubai, Tokyo, and Casablanca.

After this fifteen-year adventure, Adam decided to embark on his own ambitious enterprise, focusing on new themes. Discreet yet determined, he worked on a boutique focusing on a single genre. L'Éclair de Génie (literally, "a stroke of genius") was born, with his first boutique opening in the Marais district in Paris. Here, he worked on his concept that included éclairs of all types, chocolate bars, spreads, and chocolate candies. As this book goes to print, there are six Éclair de Génie boutiques in Paris and a number of others spread throughout Asia, in Tokyo, Yokohama, Osaka, and Kyoto, as well as Hong Kong and Seoul. Adam has authored several books, including *Éclairs*, *Tartelettes*, *Very Important Pots*, *L'Éclair de Génie*, *Caramel*, and *Workshop l'Éclair*.

In collaboration with Christophe Michalak, another star on the French pastry scene, he founded the Club des Sucrés, a club that brings together chefs from the top echelons of French pastry-making so that they can exchange their savoir-faire. Adam is also a member of the jury of the weekly TV show, *Qui Sera le Prochain Grand Pâtissier?* (Who'll be the Next Great Pastry Chef?) In addition, he is a commentator on Stéphane Bern's weekly radio show, *Comment Ca Va Bien!*, where he reveals his chef's secrets.

Last but not least, Adam is a goodwill ambassador for Rétinostop, a charity that furthers research in the fight against retinoblastoma.

**Marion
Chatelain**

**Christophe
Adam**

**Karine
Lozach**

**Sophie
Brissaud**

**Jean-Pierre
Rodrigues**

**Élise
Lepinteur**

Notes

Measuring ingredients

No pastry chef would think of working without an accurate scale in their professional kitchen, or *laboratoire*, as it is known in French. Precision is all-important to pastry chefs and in most home kitchens in France, a scale can be found. Pastry chefs even weigh liquids. Fine pastry-making is, in fact, an exact science. With the exception of ingredients in minute quantities–agar agar, pectin, and a few professional-style ingredients such as trimoline, the metric quantities for the ingredients in this book have been converted into spoon and cup volumes, with sticks and tablespoons for butter, as well as to imperial measurements. This inevitably involves some rounding-off and in most cases this does not affect the outcome. Should you want to try your hand at the more sophisticated recipes here, consider using a digital scale for accuracy. It involves minimal investment and is simplicity itself to use. You may even be won over! Of course, for spoon and cup measures, all amounts should be level, and flour must be sifted after it has been measured.

Weighing eggs

Eggs, unless otherwise specified, refer to what are called "large" eggs in North America, and "medium" in the UK. Sometimes, the outcome of a recipe depends on a precise quantity of egg—an amount that may not correspond to a whole number of eggs, or the white or yolk. To weigh out the correct amount, beat the approximate amount very lightly with a fork, just enough to break up their rather viscous structure, but no more. Place a bowl on a scale (set to zero) and gradually pour or spoon in in the correct amount.

Using gelatin sheets

Gelatin is principally available in France in the form of sheets weighing precisely 2 grams, and is the form professional bakers and pastry chefs favor. They are simple to use: soak the sheets in a little cold water until they are completely softened and rubbery (this takes five to ten minutes), then squeeze the excess water out with your hands. Transfer them to the warm or hot liquid that has to be set and stir until there are no traces of gelatin left. Do not allow the preparation to boil. Gelatin will not dissolve in a cold liquid or preparation.

How to make a dry caramel

Making caramel requires focus and attention! It is essential to use sugar that is very refined to minimize the risk of crystallization caused by impurities. A dry caramel is faster to make than one that uses water, but the process is trickier to control. Spread the sugar evenly over the base of a heavy-bottomed saucepan and place it over low to medium heat—the sugar must not cook too fast. As the edges brown and liquefy, push them toward the center using a heatproof spatula. Continue until all the sugar has colored. From this point, the caramel requires your undivided attention as the process now accelerates. As soon as the liquefied sugar is heated to the temperature specified in the recipe, or reaches the desired color, reduce the heat to low, carefully add the warmed liquid (cream, for example), and stir to combine. Keep in mind that a pale caramel will not have much taste, but a caramel that is too dark may be so bitter as to be unusable. Of course, safety is of utmost importance: hot sugar reaches temperatures that cause burns.

Useful equipment

An instant-read thermometer will take the guesswork out of heating oil—our apple fritters, page 44, are fried at 340°F (170°C) while our apple peel tempura, page 46, requires a considerably higher temperature, 400°F (200°C)—and allow you to cook a custard or pastry cream to perfection, to caramelize sugar (no more wondering if your sugar has reached the soft crack or hard crack stage), and to temper chocolate. Choose a thermometer with the widest range possible; you will also be able to use it for meats and other savory dishes.

A flexible spatula, either rubber or silicone, is an indispensible utensil for any pastry chef. Flexible spatulas are perfect for folding whisked egg whites and cream into other preparations without squashing those air bubbles, and incorporating flour into other mixtures, particularly when it is important to follow the advice not to "overmix." You can even use the flexible spatula to double as a bowl scraper to get the last traces of batter out of a mixing bowl, and they are a hygienic alternative to wooden spoons. Choose spatulas with sturdy handles, and if you can find one that is heatproof, you can use it to make caramelized preparations too.

Using Siphons

Siphons are pressurized devices and should be used with caution. Always be sure to read the safety instructions carefully before use, and check that the model you are using is compliant with the latest standards and has not been subject to a recall.

Why Use Tart Rings?

Look into any French pastry shop or bakery and you are sure to see an array of tarts, their fillings all encased in a perfectly shaped tart crust. The secret? Tart rings. With a tart ring, the base and sides are at perfect right angles, and the rim will be picture perfect. Using a tart ring may appear daunting, but it is, in fact, simple to use. To start, grease the rim of the pan with butter and place the ring over a baking sheet lined with parchment paper. When your dough is rolled very smoothly (this is essential) to a diameter large enough to fit into the ring with a little to spare, drape it over your rolling pin and unroll it over the ring. Press the dough into the lower edge of the ring all around, making sure that there aren't any pockets of air between the dough and the metal. Fit the dough in as snugly as you can without pressing on it too hard with your fingers, because if you make indentations, it will not rise evenly. Then press it very lightly against the rim. Trim the edges, either by running a knife around the top or by rolling the rolling pin over the top edge of the ring, and then follow the instructions of the recipe. When you're feeling confident enough, you can even hold the lined tart ring up in the air—the dough will stay neatly in place.

Marion Chatelain would like to thank Christophe and all the members of his team
for this most recent adventure, and Laure, for her trust.

Marion Chatelain is also very grateful to the inspiring MERCI store for its fine tableware

www.merci-merci.com
111, boulevard Beaumarchais, Paris 3ème
(pages 35, 71, 103, 121, 125, 126, 129, 135, 141, 167, 169, 171)

and to Alexandra Garrigues for her unique creations.
www.garrigues-ceramiques.com
(pages 37, 47, 49, 73, 107, 113, 173, 175)

France

Marais
43, rue Sainte-Croix-de-la-Bretonnerie
75001 Paris

BHV Marais
64, rue de Rivoli
75001 Paris

Bourse
32, rue Notre-Dame-des-Victoires
75002 Paris

Montorgueil
2, rue des Petits-Carreaux
75002 Paris

Réaumur
122, rue Montmartre
75002 Paris

Marais
14, rue Pavée
75004 Paris

Odéon
13, rue de l'Ancienne-Comédie
75006 Paris

Lafayette Gourmet
35, boulevard Haussmann
75009 Paris

L'Éclair de Génie Café
31, rue Lepic
75018 Paris

Italy

Garibaldi
Corso Garibaldi, 55
20121 Milano

La Fabrique
Corso di Porta Ticinese, 76
20123 Milano

Japan

Tokyo Nihombashi
Takashimaya Nihonbashi B1F
2-4-1 Nihonbashi, Chūō-ku
Tokyo 103-8265

Shinjuku
Takashimaya Shinjuku B1F
i5-24-2 Sendagaya, Shibuya-ku
Tokyo 151-8580

Takashimaya Yokohama B1F
1-6-31 Minamisaiwai, Nishi-ku
Yokohama 202-8601

Takashimaya Kyoto
52 Shincho, Shimogyo-ku
Kyoto 600-8001

Takashimaya Osaka
5-1-5 Nanba, Chuo-ku
Osaka 542-8510

S. Korea

Shinsegae Department Store B1
175 Shinnanpo-ro, Seocho-gu, Séoul

Hong Kong

Pacific Place, Level 2, Park Court
88 Queensway

Prince's Building Ground Floor
10 Chater Road, Central

City Super
IFC
International Finance Center Mall
Central

City Super
Times Square
1 Matheson Street, Causeway Bay

City Super
Sha Tin
New Town Plaza 1
New Town Plaza Phase-1, Sha Tin

Heartfelt thanks to Marion and Sophie, always ready to help, always good humored.
Thank you to the team at La Martinière, and to Laure in particular for her commitment to
the project.
Warm thanks to Laurent for his expert eye. And thank you also to Jean-Pierre and Élise, as
well as to Karine, dynamic, patient, and caring.

Christophe Adam

Printed in China